COMING UP ON THE ROUGH SIDE

To
Jason, Jaron, and Sister Susan,
with my love.

COMING UP ON THE ROUGH SIDE

A Black Catholic Story

MayLee Johnson

with Anne Barsanti

Published by PILLAR Books, a division of PILLAR (Pallottine Institute for Lay Leadership and Apostolate Research), Presidents Hall, Seton Hall University, South Orange, NJ 07079

Cover design: Susan Starr

Manufactured in the United States of America
92 91 90 89 88   5 4 3 2 1

ISBN 0-944734-01-4

Library of Congress Catalog Card Number: 87-63492

Contents

Preface

This book was written from my personal point of view. It tells how my life was affected by different events. It is not meant to offend or put down. It is my prayer. If the facts don't appear quite right, it's because I want it to be a prayer of my life.

There are friends I must thank: Joe Holland, Anne Barsanti, and Thomas Crowley, who kept me afloat on many a sinking day. I also want to thank my family and many others too numerous to mention. Thank you all.

Chapter 1

COMING UP
ON THE ROUGH SIDE

As I think about my childhood, I'm bothered, because I can hardly remember the really pleasant things about it. I was an outspoken, smart-mouthed, dark-skinned black girl in the sixties, and that was not good.

I've always considered myself reasonably smart. Yet no one seemed to recognize me. Being the youngest of seven kids — I have three brothers and three sisters — I often felt left out and felt that no one listened; no one talked to me. Yet they always had pet names for me like "MayLee, she's a rare bird," "She's a black sheep," "A problem child." As I think back, these names and labels became a part of me. It has taken a long time to overcome some things from my childhood.

I remember plainly how easy it was in school and making it to the fifth grade. I always enjoyed school and I read a lot. Fourth grade was very dynamic for me because I had a black teacher.

Her name was Mrs. Witherspoon. Although she appeared very thin and small, she was nothing like that in her personality. She made sure we had the basics mastered. It was always clear she cared, but she stood for no

1

nonsense. I knew what she expected from me, and I tried very hard to give it to her. She let us work to our potential and told us how really great we were. I was a fourth-grade honor student.

●

By the time I got to fifth grade, I was on a roll. I sat in the classroom and the teacher came over to me and said that I had to go to the back of the room because my desk was needed for someone else. There was an argument between us and all the kids gathered around.

It was then that I knew that I would probably be an outspoken person because I knew that injustice was being done but I was too young to really understand it. I stood in front of her and said, "It's unfair that you should treat us like this just because we're black." There was nothing I could do because she was the teacher.

I went home that night and was really upset about it, but when I tried to tell my sister, she said, "No, MayLee, it wasn't that bad." People ignored me. I sat in a corner and I did not cry but just said to myself, "I'll fix her." That's when a lot of anger began.

I told my girlfriend what had happened in our class. She said, "MayLee, that's okay." We were both in the same class, but it didn't bother her as much as it bothered me. We were so young, but I can remember a friend of mine saying, "It'll be all right. We're still smart, but no one recognizes that." I had run into my first experience of racism.

My fifth-grade teacher didn't seem to want black students in her class. It seemed as though she didn't want to teach us so she just let us play instead. One day, without notice, this teacher with her bleached red hair that was black at the roots looked at our class and said, "There are going to be some changes." She separated the black children from the white in her classroom.

I couldn't handle her attitude and her ways. I just really couldn't handle them, so I did all kinds of outrageous things to get her attention. It only caused me to get kicked out of class. I wanted to have someone to listen to me and to believe in me.

Soon the school labeled me "troublemaker," and they gave me all kinds of tests to see if I was crazy. I was confused, yet something deep inside me was always driving me to cry out, "Help me!" "Don't you care?" I wanted to be a good student like before. But from my viewpoint, the school didn't care, my parents didn't care, and the teacher obviously didn't care. I decided to play the angel and to be very nice to get the teacher to teach me. She still didn't seem interested. Simply asking her even in a nice way didn't work. It was as if she were saying, "How dare you dispute my word!"

After much complaining, she finally gave me an assignment. I was to write about what I would like to be when I grew up. I wrote I was a little black girl who became a queen. I just really loved dreaming about being a queen and carefully wrote it all down. I was to be the first black girl who became a queen. I wouldn't let anyone enter my kingdom who didn't like all children of all colors. She tore it up in my face and I cried. I grew more and more weary and wondered, "Who's listening to me?" "Who really cares about me?" My experiences in the fifth grade seem to be the root of my problems.

●

Lord, my life in school fell apart. I began to feel school was not where I wanted to be, but neither was home. My home life was not the best either.

I grew up on the poor side of South Bend, which was called the Lake. It was where all the poorer blacks lived. Most of my friends lived in the rows and rows of block-style projects. Although my family was not very rich, we lived across from the projects separated by a dirt road.

Western Avenue, a paved street, was the real dividing line. South was black, north was white. Our house and the projects were on one side and the white side was across the Lake. It was called the Lake because a polluted pond stagnated on the side of the street where the dirt road divided the poorest blacks from the poorer blacks. We were warned at an early age not to cross over into the white neighborhoods.

As a kid I used to sit and wonder why the white side looked so nice. The lawns were freshly cut and the kids were so clean. Somehow it just seemed that white was the right color and black was the wrong color. I think I turned against whites the first time because that white teacher failed me.

I always wanted to go across the street to the white side because it was really pretty. I had a friend, but she would only walk with me when we got away from both my house and her house and then we would walk together. She was blonde and had long hair and she always had a pretty ribbon in it. My mother could do my hair like that but it had to be pressed, but I didn't realize that press meant straightening.

I decided to fix my hair like my girlfriend. I went home and washed it and put all this grease in it. I braided it up but as it was drying, it got nappier and nappier. By the time my mother got home it had dried out and was matted to my head. It looked nothing like the blonde. That's when I realized that there was a difference between us. It always seemed like the white people were better, their hair always looked better or we always wanted something that was like them. I didn't want to be white, but I wanted white features.

My mother worked for a white family during all the years I was growing up. I saw two women in my mother. One would look upon the white children and smile. The other looked upon me and frowned. I could not understand it. It was really strange. I'm sure it wasn't intentional, but I used to sit back and look at that and I would wonder — really wonder.

Finally, I couldn't deal with it. I rebelled. Signals were clear to me. No one listened, cared, or tried to help me. I lost sight of school and my family.

My father used to try hard to get me to settle down, but that just didn't work out. I was in trouble with the school officials. I was a chronic offender and a runaway. Every time I ran away my friend's mother, Betty Swanson, hid me. Another time I was in trouble, my friend Pearline hid me over at her mother's house.

One time the truant officers were looking for me and I was sure I was going to be in big trouble. Pearline's mother decided to march me home. She had so many kids and she had her own problems. She knew that my father would come down to her house and go nuts.

When she took me home, she tried to put a hat on me and dress me up like a boy and told me that when I went in the house to pretend that I had amnesia. I wasn't sure what that was. She led me by the hand. We opened the door, and my father was standing in the door. He was getting ready to get me and I remember we looked up at him and said that I had amnesia. That's why I hadn't come home. I knew that I was in trouble but we thought we could fly with it. But it didn't work. I remember being walked down the street. I should have known better, but I didn't. He didn't buy it.

My parents are die-hard Christians. Do you know what

I mean? They believe that God will take care of us. I remember it was always, "I will trust in the Lord, trust in the Lord. He'll take care of you. He'll give you what you need."

I was not doing well in the fifth grade and was about to fail. I was sick of hearing about their God who cared nothing of what a young black girl thought. I wondered, "If God is so good, why isn't God giving me clothes? I mean God's not feeding us the very best." I had all these questions in my mind, but there was no one to give me any answers. I promised myself to look for the answers on my own.

•

I lost sight of school after I flunked fifth grade. I hated school. I skipped it every chance I got. I used to pull every trick in the book to get kicked out of class. You see, I was tired of fighting a system and I was beaten at home. I turned to the streets to find a place to be and some friends to be with.

The streets captured my attention fast. In the street there were black men, black women, and loads of black kids. There were Cadillacs and Lincolns, pimps and prostitutes. I loved the action in the streets. Fridays and Saturdays everyone was rocking to a beat. Once I got a taste of the life I was headed for big trouble.

Black women walked the streets day and night. Many of the women looked out for me. They taught me how to survive. The black women were beautiful beyond words. They were shaped like Coke bottles and had skin the color of smooth, dark chocolate. They would walk down the street and their thick, heavy hips rocked smoothly with their steps.

As they walked I remember hearing the howl of the

men. It was clear to me that they had captured the men's attention and had control over them. They dressed in fancy clothes, wore a lot of make-up, and loved whomever they pleased. These women were my role models. I hoped to be like them.

I decided no one really cared about me so I turned to these women. We became friends and they looked out for me. Yet, out there in those streets, I laughed and I cried. I was lonely and I was so many other things.

I have lost the words to describe it. I met trouble. In sixth grade I was removed from regular school and put in special education classes. I hardly ever went. I was surviving on the street.

The streets were my classroom, and those who lived there were my teachers.

•

Finally the school suggested to my parents I might be mentally ill. My parents gave them permission to test me again. I resented the people at school for testing me. It seemed like only whites tested me and talked down to me and had no concern for my feelings. I was just put out with school.

Home was no better. I was beaten at home. I hated the beatings so much it seemed that the streets were safer and more peaceful. My father would beat me for anything, but he could never beat me silent because I tried to believe in the Lord that he gave me.

By the time I was supposed to be in eighth grade I was totally blown. I didn't know what to do. I didn't want to leave the streets, but my parents and school officials wouldn't let me stay there. I was placed in detention. I was in and out of the detention center.

I didn't know who to turn to. My parents were totally

unaware of all the problems I was facing. They often sided with school officials, and because of that, they lost me. I had been kicked out of all the schools in South Bend and Mishawaka. At fourteen, my life was hell.

●

I was suspended from public school property and was arrested for being there. Finally they sent me to Indiana Girls School for robbing a pop truck.

I thought a lot on my trip down to the school. All these things happened to me because I wanted to be someone. I wanted to learn but no one was there to teach me. I wanted to be a student, but I hated school and was afraid. I didn't want to be a black girl that no one cared about. I wanted to die.

Indiana Girls School was my home for six months. It was a place I will never forget. I remember when I first walked in there and the walls were so dead-gray looking, and everything was so big and institutional. I was in the kitchen. I hadn't even been there six hours before the warden walked in front of me and told me, "You're going to do whatever I want you to do. If I tell you to get undressed and just stand here you're going to do it." I thought to myself, "No, I'm not going to do it."

Before nightfall on the first day I was there, I was in solitary. I had taken a metal pitcher that we dipped milk out of and hit the warden in the head. With that I was able to hold my own ground after being locked up in there and not having to depend on anyone. I was tough. Plus I had a cousin and two friends in there at the same time.

The walls were puke-green, the beds were iron, and the wardens were white women. There were always two women to oversee forty girls. Twenty beds lined each side of a long, dark hallway. At night, when the lights were out, we all cried uncontrollably. I used to get up at night and walk down the aisles and hold my crying friends. Some of us cared for each other. We were a family of sorts.

It was a cold place. The coldest I have ever been. Some of the girls were in for murder or stealing, and most were runaways. It was a very sad time, but I lived through it — never forgetting a moment.

I didn't believe in myself. I thought I was nothing. I felt like nothing, and no one seemed to care. No one told me, "MayLee, you're okay." They just let me know if I did anything wrong. And if I did something wrong I got a beating. I took so many beatings — so many beatings for being mouthy, but I wasn't being mouthy. I was just saying, "I have a right to speak!" "I have a right to say things, and I have a right to say something."

In that god-awful place, my body was abused, I was medicated, and I had to learn to be hard core. Where was this God I needed to ease my pain?

While I was in solitary confinement, I made up little songs like this:

> *Jesus I love you,*
> *yes I do.*
> *I love you Jesus,*
> *I hope you love me too.*

I was locked up in solitary for a couple of months, and they put me in a rubber room. It was padded; no one was there with me and I used to sit in there and think. Finally I couldn't take it anymore, and I just gave in to the fact that I was nothing.

I lived daily in constant fear and trusted no one. I forget the ages, the faces, the people, and places. I just gave up. An eighth-grader giving up!

Even so, I'd sing to myself. I'd sing these songs, and

it seemed like the pain would go away. It just didn't hurt as much when I sang. I always had a deep spiritual something. I had a one-to-one relationship with the Lord — as I think about it now. I used to talk to him all the time. When I was locked up somewhere and couldn't get out, I would sing:

> *These old bars can't hold me.*
> *Only you can, my Lord.*
> *I wish that you would help,*
> *because I'm so very sore.*

I took so many beatings. I took so many licks and knocks to get some sense into me. I began to believe what people were saying about me. "She's weird." "She's strange." "She's different." I would say, "Please, Jesus, why is it so rough with me? Why can't I just be me?"

Being in Girls School did not help me, but it did succeed in hardening my heart.

•

I was released from Girls School earlier than I expected because a priest friend of mine spoke for me. My friends on the street told Father Daniel Piel where I was. He came down a few times to talk with me. It was a long process. Back in South Bend, I headed for the street until my parents could decide where to send me to school. I continued to rely on the streets for food and friends.

One day I was sitting around thinking I should be in school but no school would accept me, so I was just walking around the streets. I was on Washington Street. I needed to walk down this street because at least one person would recognize me and ask where I had been.

Washington Street was just vacant houses, prostitutes, pimps, drugs. But right in the middle of Washington Street was a recreation center where everybody went in and had drinks and shared conversation and laughed and talked. And if someone was looking to pick someone up, it was probably in that recreation center. Even in the midst of all the bad of Washington Street, there was a place where you could walk in and meet a friend and talk to the people. Washington Street was never closed. Whatever you went looking for on Washington Street, you could always find it.

Washington Street was also the worst street in South Bend. Every minute there were murders, rapes, and fights. To walk down the street was dangerous. The buildings on Washington looked like they had gone through a World War II bomb raid. The destroyed houses held broken memories and lost people. Yet the street was alive, never empty. There were groups of black men and women standing and laughing and talking. For so many, like me, the street was home and family.

I was cooling out and looking for somebody to talk to or someone to get drunk with, but no one was around. I was just walking along, lost and feeling like a motherless child. There's a song that I sang a lot when I was young and messed up. I would sit down and the words would pop into my mind. I discovered later that a song is a prayer so, in fact, I was praying all the time. The song's mellow tune and soft words had a soothing effect on me:

> *Sometimes I feel like a motherless child.*
> *Sometimes I feel like a motherless child.*
> *Sometimes I feel like a motherless child*
> *a long way from home.*

I remember I sang it that day.

It was so strange that day. I had recently been released, and I wasn't used to being free, to going where I pleased. I needed a place to go and just cool out. I had another chance at freedom and I didn't want to blow it. I was staying low because most of the police knew me, and they knew I had troubles.

I ran up to this house just off Washington Street. It was a regular house. I knew it was a place to go. I didn't want to go home. So I went up the stoop, knocked, and said, "Excuse me, can you help me? I don't know what to do and I have nobody to turn to." A very tall, lean white lady came to the door and just looked at me for a moment. She said, "Please, come in."

I went in the St. Peter Claver House. The House had opened its doors to poor black families who lived on the West Side of town (this includes Washington Street). It invited all who needed help into a Christian environment to learn about living simply and loving your neighbors and friends. At the time I entered the St. Peter Claver House, I was a very troubled young girl. Mrs. Edith Kyler was the tall lean lady. She cared for me at first sight. She also told me the place belonged to all of us.

There were always a lot of people moving about in the House — students from Notre Dame and St. Mary's, seminarians, priests, and nuns. All were willing to give some time.

There was warmth in the House. I felt peace was there. It was a place I learned about Jesus and the saints of the church. I remember seeing a picture of Jesus, but I didn't know it was Jesus. Later I realized it was surely Jesus because he loves the poor. This was a house where people came and they had a place to sit and talk.

The St. Peter Claver House became my home after Girls school. It was a place I could go if I didn't understand a math problem, if I had a problem at school, or if I was hungry. I was so lucky because if I needed someone to talk to, Mrs. Kyler was there to listen or she would get someone. She ran the St. Peter Claver House. She was just a regular lady that cared for people. Mrs. Kyler was very much a role model for me during those times.

I still remember most of the people that I met at the House. Some are still very much a part of my life. I had found happiness at the House and never wanted to lose it. At the House I could get away from the pressures of having always been a bad girl. I found a place of peace.

Father Dan Piel became my friend. He openly loved and cared for black children. As pastor of St. Augustine's, the only black church in South Bend, he cared for all people both black and white. And he had a special love for youth. He opened a new life for me. I began to trust his teaching, and he baptized me in the Catholic church. With his help I returned to school.

●

My teen-age years were very difficult, but Father Piel convinced me I must continue. I had matured but there was still a long way to go. I began to talk with him and share with him how terrible it was for me growing up. I told him I had no one to listen to me. I had been beaten, and through it all no one was out there to tell me that I would be okay. Father Piel often sat for hours and listened.

He promised me that in a little while my life would change and the labels I had known would later change my life. I didn't want to be a rare bird when I was young. I was hearing all bad things in the names they called me and I was believing them. I didn't realize that those names also describe a strong, independent person. I am still learning about myself.

We were all gathered at the St. Peter Claver House and

Father Piel came in and said that St. Joe's High School was looking to take some black students into their freshman class of 1966. He sent six of us over to take the test. I was out somewhere so I missed it when the kids got together and decided to take the test and fail it.

I went in there and they gave us the test and I worked really hard. What the school wanted at the time was black kids that they thought would be academically able to handle the curriculum at St. Joe's High School. I was always a reader and always felt that I knew something. I took the test and I passed it and I was accepted there. Once my parents found out that I had taken the test and was accepted, they said I was going. My other friends did so poorly they were not chosen.

St. Joe's was a very fine school — a place where the Sisters of Holy Cross looked after me. Father Piel brought me to these sisters and gave me to them and told them he'd dig up the money if they could teach me. He became my sponsor. The love and the strength they showed me helped a lot. The sisters were tough and strict with discipline but very understanding.

Sister Angela later told me she fought like holy hell to keep me in St. Joe's. The challenge of being with those kids and in that school brought me out of my thinking that I was nothing. St. Joe's kids didn't seem to care where I came from or where I had been. Yet I spent so much time being jealous of them because I felt I wasn't as smart as they were until again I failed.

Freshman year was a time of adjustment, and I had an attitude problem. Sister Dominick was really naive and we would really do rotten things to her. We were in religion class and she went out of the room for something, so we threw raisins all over her desk. We put raisins everywhere. When she came into the class, she looked around and saw all the raisins and got really scared. She said, "My God, what is this?" We told her they were dead flies, and she believed us.

She also believed the stories that I used to tell her. The reason I did not hand any homework in was because my mother and father would beat me and they would tie me to the bed post. She got smart one day and called them and found out that I wasn't telling the truth. Then I was in big trouble.

I thought I was dumb, and I failed myself. I never studied in my freshman and sophomore years. I just sat and felt sorry for myself. I was just so used to not believing in myself that I willed myself to fail. So there I was again in a different place, a different time, a different school, and confused. It was becoming clearer to me every day that I was different from the other kids at school.

I wondered why. Why was I poor and they were rich? Why was I black? The rough truth was that I grew up "on the rough side."

•

I was living in two worlds — rough and poor, smooth and rich. I went to school with rich white kids who dressed very nicely, drove nice cars, traveled around the country and world. It all seemed so natural and smooth that you should have all these things. I was very jealous and unhappy about being a poor black girl in a rich fancy school. I was very confused.

I was obsessed with becoming one of these kids, but I was not dressing the part. So I would beg, borrow, and steal to look like they did. But I soon discovered there wasn't enough that could make me one of them.

I returned to the real side of my life — the streets and my friends. Some of my friends had left school to have babies and some were working in the streets.

I was a junior at St. Joe's, and I ran a house of prostitution on weekends to make money to buy clothes to look like the other St. Joe's kids. I was working as a part-time madam along with the desk clerk at the LaSalle Hotel. We managed a pretty good business. We treated the girls, my friends, with as much care and respect as we could for the business we were in. The girls often made enough money in one hour to feed, clothe, and buy presents for their children.

It was not a pretty time in my life. I was confused. I was taught in school about my body being a temple of the Holy Spirit but I saw street life where bodies and lives were beaten and bruised. I couldn't stand the idea of undressing for men's pleasures, but if I wanted to continue I had to find a way. That's how I became the manager.

We were soon run out of business after Momma Chicky discovered me. I was getting her business. She was the head street madam. My girls only needed to work two days, three tricks a night. It was a clean set up. Momma Chicky loved to hate me. She put a contract out on me.

Fortunately, Father Piel found out and sent me to live with his friends in Fort Wayne for five months. At least I had new clothes and I could fit right in with the rich St. Joseph's students. It's funny to think that Momma Chicky was a Catholic from Louisiana. Father Piel bailed me out of trouble with her. He explained to her that I was a confused young girl, and so she decided not to kill me.

After that business I went back to St. Joe's to finish school. The kids there knew nothing of my other life. I was in my senior year in high school.

•

Yes, it's been rough, it's been hard, and it's been a lesson for me. It's been such a lesson because now I can believe in myself, rely on myself, and rely on my merit. Now instead of pitying myself, saying: "I'm a poor black girl, so I can't do it," I began to believe that I could do it.

Sister John reassured me that I could do it and I would make it. She knew everything about me. Sister John Joseph was a heavy-set, round-faced, and usually jovial Dean of Girls. She wore a black habit and a veil that looked like a paper plate. She knew about my family problems, history, and my personal life as a "manager." Yet when I was to be out of town by sundown, she along with Father Piel saw to it that I was safe. She taught me about the saints and would spend hours talking with me.

But I thought I was so smart. I thought I could use her and do whatever I pleased. One day she had to discipline me for not handing in an assignment. I thought I could yell at her and call her what I pleased. I was no saint. I was in for a rude awakening. She slammed me up against the brick wall, and I must have been two feet off the ground when she told me in no uncertain language to straighten up. I did. Case closed. Sister John saw me through a very tough few years in high school.

I was pleased to be able to be a student at St. Joe's and I began to feel like, Wow, I'm saved! I can do it. I went back to tell Mrs. Kyler and everybody at the House that I was going to make it in school. It was going to be wonderful, yet I found that my happy news was met with their sad news.

The House was going to be closing and along with it, my support. There went my security. I was so afraid of losing them and especially their support. I cried to think that the St. Peter Claver House was closing. I was so afraid of what was going to happen.

It seemed like nothing ever came easy for me and a lot of my strength during that time was drawn from the saints. I had been introduced to the lives of the saints in high school. Their stories and their lives became my backbone. St. Augustine and, oh! Joan of Arc, my God, they burned her at the stake! This woman had to have strength. Canonizing her just doesn't seem enough.

Sources of my strength also came from people like Father Piel and Mrs. Kyler, the sisters and the students at St. Joseph's, the people at the House who took time to help me as well as my friends. I could also sing a song and it would remove some of my fears. I was more determined now then ever to make it. Although the House had closed I had not. I received so much from that place.

•

I began to realize there were some caring people because someone had cared for me. I had spent so much of my life scared, but now I didn't need to be afraid. Once again, through the grace of God, through my little songs and through my determination that there is a better life for me, I watched the ups and downs of it all. I held in there and persevered and I made it. As a senior in high school I realized that life is not fair and it's not easy. It wasn't easy for a black girl who's been through a world of trouble before she got there. I was the black girl who had hardship, who was what you call a throwaway.

Many people thought I simply should not be in the school and it worried me a lot, so I have to thank those who believed in me and saw me through it to the end and graduation. Now I am a believer in man, woman, and Christ. As I remember, I sing:

> *I'm coming up on the rough side of the mountain,*
> *but I got a hold to God's unchanging hand.*
> *I'm coming up on the rough side of the mountain,*
> *I'm doing my best to understand.*

Chapter 2

LORD, HELP ME
TO HOLD OUT

I was not like other students who were college material.
They all had plans to go to different colleges. I just wanted
to graduate from St. Joe's. We didn't have enough money
for me to attend a college but I wondered what I would
do next. I wasn't a serious student. I was just getting
through school — trying so hard to do something but all
the time not really sure what I was trying to do or what
I really wanted for myself. I had poor study habits and
skills and few goals.

When I was about ready to graduate from St. Joe's
we had to make some decisions on what we wanted to
be and I did not even think about college. I was a little
shocked when I got out of St. Joe's High School and there
were different colleges that were offering me a chance to
come. It was interesting because I was never motivated
for college. I decided to go to a college in Washington,
D.C. — Howard University. Often I don't even say that
I went there because all I did was just pass through the
doors. But that's where I registered.

Strangely enough I applied and got accepted. Of course
you've got to go if you're accepted. My parents were pretty

decent about it. They were willing to help me if I wanted
to help myself.

At school I met some girls who were from different
parts of the country. They were like me, not great students, but having to be there to please their parents or
because of expectations.

Four of us registered together, and then we found out
that we were too late for on-campus housing. So we had to
live off campus in an apartment. Jerretta, Betty, Sandy,
and I moved into an apartment together. We were four
girls looking for a good time in D.C., and we used college
for it.

●

Jerretta was a beautiful dark brown girl from North Car-
olina. She cooked and kept house. I thought she was
insecure and had been over-protected. Sandy was a "high
yellow." She was pretty, and she knew it, and she made
sure we all knew it too. We called Sandy a "lemon twister"
because when she walked she moved so much it left a sour
taste in our mouths. Betty was cocoa brown, with big sad
eyes. She was homely looking. She never smiled and was
never happy until we were partying or some of her male
friends were lying to her in her face. We were a rare group
trying to share a small apartment, dreams, and experiences that each of us would long remember.

I noticed that beauty was a value for many of the girls.
Physical beauty was number one with a couple of my room-
mates. Betty and I were friends from South Bend so we
knew each other and we decided we were not beautiful
women and probably would not be popular at college. I
think that was part of our downfall. The two of us shared
negative feelings about ourselves. The others were definitely high on beauty, and they were beautiful.

We had been living together for maybe six months and Jerretta was the only one going to classes regularly. Jerretta was the typical story, but it wasn't typical to us because we were not used to it. She was going to school and she met a really super guy. They were good friends, yet he came to ruin her. Everything that she wanted or everything she thought she wanted was wrapped up in him. He was a "super jock" and would come to our apartment. He would sit down and eat up our food. We cared about her and decided to let her get away with it for a time.

Being who I am, I decided that enough was enough and just straight up told him that he had to leave and find another hangout because there were four women in this house. We liked to come home and relax. We didn't want to be beholden to some jerk who comes along and eats our food. This brought conflict among us, and Jerretta was a little resentful.

Eventually she came around and she listened and she saw that enough is enough. We really liked her. She had so much going for her.

At the time, there was a lot of LSD, a lot of drugs. Reefer has always been around, but LSD was the party drug. Everyone had to take a trip. If you hadn't taken the ultimate trip you were jive. I skipped the ultimate trip but Jerretta didn't. She came home a couple of nights really spaced out. People were dropping LSD in drinks. So we were always warning each other to be careful about what we drank.

Jerretta didn't take heed, and she continued to go out with the jerk. He eventually dropped out of school, and she decided to go wherever he went because she was so in love with him. One night she came home and was really depressed. She was also really high. Everybody got out of bed and we took care of her. She was confused, very wet with sweat, and very much pregnant.

We talked to her and we told her we cared even if he didn't. I guess he decided that he didn't want to date anymore. He knew she was pregnant. She just couldn't handle the rejection. We talked to her and we tried to bring her down and we gave her milk. We stayed up half the night until we were all exhausted. Finally we thought she had fallen asleep. So we all went to bed thinking that she'd be okay and we'd check on her in the morning. Well, that night she jumped off the balcony.

It was the ultimate blow because I really thought she was okay that night, but she was dead the next morning.

We were not sure what to do or say. We were shocked and very upset. Someone had to contact her parents. We were all afraid. I called her parents and told them that their daughter just bailed off the fourth floor balcony and was dead. Our roommate, a person who lived with us daily, was dead. Of course they said it was drug related. Her family took her back home and buried her.

•

Our house fell apart. I could not handle it. I didn't know what to do, so I had to get out of there. Her memories kept playing in my head.

None of us had a real close relationship with our parents. No one had a real close friend to talk to, so it was just the three of us — no one being superior to the others — we were equals. We didn't know exactly what to do. I remember so well saying, "Lord, help me to hold on, I don't know what's going on."

I packed my bags to go back to South Bend. There was nowhere for me because I had no place to go. I could go back to my parent's house yet I knew that within a matter of time I would have to leave it again.

We had not talked about what happened. It was like

we wanted to keep it quiet. There was a lot going on. I sat in the airport all by myself waiting for the plane to come and take me back home. I was so sure that I was going back home to nothing. I sat there with just one suitcase. I hardly had any clothes. It was so expensive living in Washington. I was flying home not really sure what I was going back to. I felt so empty, feeling like I left something that I didn't know anything about. I was going home where no one was expecting me back. I knew that I was headed for trouble as soon as I got off the plane in South Bend.

There she was, Pearline, to pick me up in her old jalopy. She took me to her house and we sat there. I told her everything. The table legs were shaky and there were kids screaming all around, but I went back there. She said, "Well, May, you know how it is. You can stay here until you get yourself together." I got in a lot of trouble because of Pearline but there was a bond between us. She was always around to cushion the fall. We're still friends. Every time I slipped and fell, there was always a friend I could go to.

I arrived in South Bend a college failure. I had just left the only place I might have had a chance of succeeding, and I found myself right back where all my troubles began. I couldn't hang with the fast life so I just came back home. I had nothing to come back to — nothing. It was a negative comeback, on top of severe depression. This, too, became a struggle in my life. I stayed with Pearline, while I looked for a job and tried to find my own way. People would take me in, but I had to find something for myself.

I always went back to Pearline's. She would take me in and tell me, "Things are going to be okay, MayLee, just hang in there." Then she would say, "You get the dinner tonight." I would fix the dinner and it was okay, but I had to go out and get a job. I worked. I always worked, but I never worked a job that was pleasing to me. I had different jobs as a nurse's aid and in nursing homes and hospitals. I just worked and made money and lived.

I was just existing. I think it's important that you don't just exist. I think it is important that somehow you keep moving and that's how it was with me. I kept moving and I kept singing. Working saved my sanity, and music saved my soul.

I always sang. It has only been in the last few years that I've learned that as I was singing, I was praying. Singing was such a way for me to release tension. I would pray, "What am I supposed to do, Lord?"

•

I was beginning to get older and all my friends had kids and I had nothing. I had to find the ultimate lover, I thought. It was so tacky because I didn't realize what I really had. To me, at that time in my life, I felt something was missing, and I just didn't know what to do. Someone introduced me to a guy that I really didn't like, but I brought myself to like him. I needed someone and I didn't want to be alone in life.

The first thing I learned as a black woman is that I am very gullible. Also, in my community, women without men are automatically labeled something negative, and I did not need another label tacked to me.

I became a woman who had a passion for seeking a man. I didn't care who he was as long as he wasn't crazy. I didn't care as long as I had somebody.

I ran into the guy who eventually became my first son's father. It was a loveless relationship. I was existing with him, not even caring, sexually, physically, just being there, and I became such an actor. I could act out the part of the happy, wonderful girlfriend. I could be all the things for my son's father, but I was losing myself. I had to forget who I was. I wasn't important. I just satisfied a need. This guy would drink and then he would come over. He would get drunk and then he would come over to talk to me about love.

"How much did he love me?" I kept thinking, "I'm getting older." I was about twenty-four or twenty-five years old. I wanted a baby and I thought, "I better have a baby." Something inside me said, "But you don't need a baby." I'd ride the buses and everybody would have their little kid. I've got to have a baby of my own. Since I know this guy's pretty decent, he's who I will have my baby by. It wasn't like a trick or anything. I talked to him about it. He wanted to be a father.

He said he was sure he wanted to be a father. He said, "I want to have this baby with you and we are going to be the perfect family. We are going to have a house; we're going to be married; we're going to be happy and have all the things you want." What a lie...

•

As soon as I was pregnant things changed instantly. Here I was thinking, "Okay, we're going to get married, we're going to have a happy home, and we'll be together." Well, things changed, and things that had never mattered before became a problem. I was too fat, I was too dark. Always something wrong. I spent a lot of time trying to redo all these things.

I went on a diet by taking pills to try to lose weight because there was no way I could train myself to go on a diet. I just needed the pills. I'd go to the streets to get speeders. You can drop them and you can lose the weight. I lost weight, but that wasn't right. I dyed my hair. I did all these things to be appealing to him. I didn't like all the changes, but I just didn't want to be by myself, and I didn't want to have a baby without someone.

I thought we had made a mutual agreement about the baby. It was 1975. I became pregnant, I had this baby, and I want you to know the same man who came and spent numerous nights at my apartment and planned with me to have this baby stood up in a court of law three times and told the judge, "It's not my baby."

The first time we went to the courthouse I was very hesitant, but I had no choice with no source of income. I applied for AFDC (Aid for Dependent Children). To apply for AFDC you have to prosecute the father. I figured that would be no sweat because, of course, he loved me and we were going to get married and be happy. Well, when I told him what I had to do he became hostile. "Who said this is my baby?" The shock of that really hurt me. I thought, "My God, of course it's his baby!" I spent the last two years with this guy and I know that this is his baby. But I needed the money, and so I went through all the legal processes.

•

Let me tell you what the court system does to a poor black woman. The judge was nasty to me. I thought it would be the other way around. I thought he would rip this guy's head off for lying about fathering the baby. The judge asked me questions like: "Are you sure this is the father?" "How many times did you have this guy?" "Where did you have him?" "How many other guys did you have?"

I was totally insulted, but I wouldn't cry and I didn't give in. Something inside me said, "MayLee, hold on." I listened and didn't say anything. Finally I said, "Well, sir, I'm not sure that I can document all the times because I have been with the guy two years but I am sure that this is his baby." Okay, well that's not good enough. But the guy says it's not his so we have to run blood tests.

I was appalled at the thought of having to have my baby tested by the court to get the father to pay money. I went to him and I said, "Could you tell me what's wrong? All of a sudden you don't want the baby?" He insisted, "This ain't none of my baby." That was really appalling to me and I said to myself, "I don't need him. Forget it, I'm leaving."

But I went back and I tried the courts again. The judge this time said. "Okay, bring the baby in and we'll have it tested." Again, I just said, "Forget it I'm not going to go through it."

I've always been a survivor. When I say survivor, I mean just that. I have always had a hard time, but I've managed to survive. It was starting to seem that no matter how much I tried or believed, I would never quite succeed. With one kid I can make it, so I refused to go back to court the third time. But the father's mother convinced me to continue. She told him, "You shouldn't lie like that. You really ought to claim the baby." She really helped me. She was determined it was his baby.

I knew that it was his child, but I had been through so much and it hurt so bad. Once again I felt like nothing; I felt like dirt. I didn't think that I should be the one to feel terrible for what had happened but of course not being married and being single, "It's the mother's baby; the daddy's maybe." That's how it was always told to me. And that's how it is.

•

So I had made up my mind that I would just work and support the baby. I got my mother to keep him and finally one day I got a letter saying that Jason's father had signed the paternity papers. They told him to pay me $17.50 a week.

Well, that settled that, and I was through with this guy. My baby was a few months old, maybe four months, and I was pregnant again with someone I was rebounding with. I was out of control. I couldn't believe how stupid I was. I had just been through hell, and now on the damned rebound, I had to blow it again.

I thought about jumping off buildings. I thought of all kinds of things to abort this baby. I just could not believe that I was so stupid and neither could anybody else. No one let me live it down. I was pregnant again. I tried to hide it, but I couldn't hide, and I just didn't have the guts to tell anybody. I was so ashamed of myself. I really hated myself.

I said, "How could you do this to yourself, MayLee?" "What is wrong with you?" "You're not loving anybody. You're just satisfying a need that's not even being satisfied." Whether it was the need or the insecurity, I'm not sure. I figured it was the insecurity, and I told myself, "Enough is enough."

I had another beautiful baby boy. I loved him. He was chunky, sweet Jaron. My babies, Jason and Jaron, are the best things that ever happened to me.

●

My problems didn't go away. I was still very confused. I had two children thirteen months apart. Two babies in pampers, two babies drinking milk. Two babies to feed, to clothe, and I had to do it all on AFDC. I was losing it. I was losing control of my life, I was losing control of taking care of my kids.

I went from a failure at college back to the streets of South Bend, to an instant mother, then a mother of two.

Two live, breathing human beings who needed me. I cried and prayed. "Lord, what am I doing? Help me."

But there was no one to help me. I tried my best to be a good mother, but I did not really know how. I had double problems, and I was not sure how to handle both babies. I tried to meet their every need. I didn't want the boys to cry, to be wet, or to need anything. My whole life belonged to them. I completely forgot my friends. I never wanted my boys out of my sight.

Next door to me I had a girlfriend. We lived in the projects. She had a little boy at the same time that I had a little boy. Her baby died of Sudden Infant Death Syndrome. I went crazy. I wouldn't let Jason out of my sight. I stayed with him half the night. Nothing ever happened to him. He had a lot of holding, so he just stuck with me. I regret making a baby like that because no one could keep him and he would have to stay with me all the time. He's growing into a good young man.

There was one problem that eventually caused me to head toward a nervous breakdown. Jaron and Jason had their nights and days mixed up, so I was up twenty-four hours a day. I began taking speed again to help me stay awake, and it was too much.

"What am I going to do?" I just couldn't handle it anymore. So I took the kids over to my mother's and I split. I dumped these two babies on a family who I thought didn't care for me. They took care of these kids while I went around to try to find myself. I began to see a pattern. Whenever the going got tough, I ran away. I went to the streets looking for help. I stayed with my friend Pearline and a few others. We've been together since childhood. Throughout my life, my friends have been such a cushion.

I sat somewhere and I cried and I thought, "Poor me, poor MayLee who has all these problems. Nobody cares." I was holding a pity party for myself and I loved it, because

I could sit there and tell myself over and over again, "It's not my fault, it's not my fault. It's someone else's fault." It was my way to escape. I left my kids with my mother; my family was taking care of them and I was not. No one ever came looking for me to bring the kids back to me. They just let me go out to find myself.

My dad told me, "You can run up and down the street all you want, but you're not going to run up and down the street with these kids. They need to be somewhere." My mother and my father and my sister took care of the kids until I could find myself.

•

It wasn't until I hit the rock bottom in the street, in a ditch, that I met up with Mable. I had been in the streets a couple of months. Today we would call Mable a bag lady. She was a street woman. I remember I was so drunk. I was just sitting looking like a drunk. No control — no nothing — just out there. She sat beside me and began to talk to me. I said, "Mable, why do you think life is so bad for us?" She said, "MayLee, lots of times we make our own life bad because we don't know what's good when it's good. Somehow you have to make the good work for you."

She didn't really know what she meant. She was just trying to console me. I said, "Well you don't have anything to be happy about. You live out here. You don't have anything." She responded, "I don't see you jumping for joy, you don't have anything either." I said, "Yes, I do. I have two kids." Then she said, "Well, you ain't got them here." I said, "No, my mother has them and is taking care of them because I'm having problems."

"Let me tell you something about problems," she said. "Problems are always going to be here, but you better get your butt home and see about those kids because they're not your mother's responsibility. It's good that you've got a mother that's willing to watch them, but she's raised her kids and she don't need to be saddled down with her daughter's kids. You got to go and take responsibility for what's your own." She continued, "I raised four kids who have grown and they all left me. Nobody took care of me." She thought she wasn't a mother for them, but she felt she was the best she could be.

"You still got time to save them, MayLee, and if it means going to the bottom and not having them, then it's not worth it. You must be at the bottom of the slide. But don't leave your children. There's nothing worse than being alone." I was left sitting there — thinking and praying, "What can I do? How can I? It's too hard. I don't want to do it. I don't know what to do."

•

So I sat there and felt sorry for myself. Finally I went over to my mother's house and said, "Well, I'll take the kids." She said, "No. You've got to have a house and a place for these kids to go because I'm not just turning them over to you. The next thing I know you'll be right back." She said, "No!"

I went walking around and met Reverend Kirk, a Baptist preacher. He ran the LaSalle Park Houses — project houses around the Lake — where I grew up. I talked to him, and he gave me a house with two bedrooms at $57 a month. He let me move in for nothing. Nothing! And he gave me a couch to sleep on my first night. I didn't have any money or anything but he just said, "Okay, you move in and then when you get settled you can pay me the deposit and the back rent."

So it was like someone's always looking out for me so that I could have another chance. I moved into this project

house, and there was nothing in the house when I moved
in except the couch. My mother gave me two baby beds
for the children. I remember it was a Friday when I picked
up the kids, and we moved into the project. That's when I
decided to make a commitment to the kids to try to raise
them, to try to take care of them, and to try to teach
them. There have been many times I wanted to run away.

It was hard but I was no longer afraid. I believed I
could do it. I would never again defeat myself before I
tried. I moved into the house with the kids and we looked
after each other. They have had an amazing impact on
my life. They have helped to mold me into who I am.

Jason, my first-born, was born in 1975. I knew he
would be very sensitive. I never let anyone see me cry, but
I cried every day that I carried this baby. I cried when
people were not looking, because I didn't know what my
life was going to be like. I was really worried and bothered
that I couldn't be a good mother to him. I was scared that
he would feel like I felt — that no one loved him. The guy
didn't want him, and I was beginning to think that I didn't
want him.

He was born and he was mine. He wasn't a perfect
baby; he had a big knot on his head. His head was really
not well-rounded. The doctor said it was because he had
knocked up against my pelvis. I love him. He knows that.
He's very close to me. As a young baby, he walked at
seven months. He became the big brother soon after that
because I had my son Jaron only a year later. I had two
babies in two years and I was a single mother.

I sat on my couch and put Jaron in my lap and Jason
on the couch. We bumped so much on the couch until one
day the whole back of the couch fell out. We all fell on the
floor and we had some lumps, but that was so funny. We
were happy to be together.

Jason's sensitive, he's smart, and he's always eager to

know what is going on. He is precious. He would tell me, "Don't cry, Mom." When I was pregnant with Jaron, Jason became really close to me. He stayed with me, and he would cry. There were only three people that could keep Jason — my mother, my mother's friend, and once in a while my sister's husband. Those were the only three people that Jason would stay with because we were just so close. I didn't want anything to happen to him so I held him all the time.

Although he continues to get better, at times he is still very insecure. Yet at times that I've needed him most the strong part of him that always wants to take charge comes through. He is a young man and I am very proud of him. I am sure he will make it.

Jaron came in with as much love from me as Jason did. He was ten pounds and he was like a Pillsbury Doughboy. I love him madly. Jaron was so easy to care for because he always had company with Jason. He was never lonely and Jason watched over him just as well as anybody could. They were very close. Jaron is the one that would just walk up to you and give you a hug for nothing and you'd give him one back.

Jaron is very independent, where Jason is more dependent on me. Jaron would sit and play by himself. Both of their personalities would even it out. If one was acting up, the other one wouldn't.

Jaron is the opposite of me and Jason. Jaron's strong, he's sensitive (but you won't know it). He will stand tall. He is loving and wonderful, and so sincere.

•

Our being together gave me time to feel out their personalities. I got a chance to watch them grow, to take care of them, to clean them. We were not rich. We were poor.

But the three of us were in our own house even if it was not the best place. We cared very much for each other.

There were roaches and rats running all over everywhere, but we tried to make the best of every situation and to take care of each other. They were growing into pretty good kids. They were very sensitive and very much aware of what it was like to be poor, but they didn't let it hold them back. They learn quickly. The most important thing to remember is we were a family.

We were going to work as a family — to be a family. And maybe we weren't the best family, but we made it a commitment. I remember so plainly. Jason and Jaron had turned three and two. I talked to them about whether they wanted to go to day care, because I needed to go to work. I said, "You need to go to day care and day care will be big fun." We talked about it. This turn in my life was triggered by a home visit from a white social worker. The woman came to interview me and the kids to qualify for AFDC. She seemed a little surprised and made a comment, "What clean little kids." After the visit Jason said, "I don't want to do that any more."

Mrs. Ivy ran the best day care center in the community. She made sure that the children were loved. Jason and Jaron were really thrilled about going to day care so I could go to work. They waited for the bus each morning. It was like we were beginning to grow and we were taking steps toward living. We didn't know we were growing. We just began to take control of our lives and we grew.

They went to school and I went to work. I had taken a job at a nursing home. We continued to live much like anybody else. But there was always that commitment to each other. It was a pact that we made when they were little: "To care for each other no matter what, to be friends with each other no matter what." And if something comes up or someone does something to us, we tell each other.

We never hold any secrets. We promised that we would love each other.

The projects were not the best place to live. We promised each other that we would tell everything if anything happened. If someone touched them in the wrong place or anything that they sensed was not right they should confide in me. Fortunately, all went well.

I remember telling them that years ago, and it has stayed with them. I think because of that they began to be okay. But then again, there was something not quite right within my life. This was a restless period. Whenever it was time for me to move or for me to grow there was always an inner drive in me. It was pushing me saying, "Okay, you've got here, but there is more."

Although my life was still not the best it was shaping up. I had no real direction. I worked hard to raise my family, but the kids were turning into little savages. I just knew that I had to move from the projects. I kept working, and I didn't know when I would be able to move, but I had to go.

Finally, I got another job at the hospital that was paying pretty reasonable money. It was time for me to leave the projects. I had saved some money but it wasn't quite enough. My friends Pearline and Marie helped out. They loaned me some money for the move. We moved from the projects into a one-bedroom apartment that was on a quiet side of town, a quiet side of Studebaker with the kids' day care center right down the street. I said,

> *Lord, help me to hold out,*
> *Lord, help me to hold out,*
> *Lord, please help me to hold out*
> *Until the change I'm looking for comes.*

Chapter 3

PRECIOUS LORD, TAKE MY HAND

Precious Lord, take my hand,
Lead me on, let me stand,
I am tired, I am weak, I am worn.

Jim Dorsey wrote this song. He was away at a convention when he got the word to come home right away. He got home and found his wife and baby were dead. His wife died in childbirth. In his grief he wrote the words to "Precious Lord." He had hit the bottom when he lost everyone close to him.

"Precious Lord" has special meaning for me because it's a song that makes a way out of no way. When something in your life is missing, the words offer relief to a weary soul — yet not without a lot of suffering, pain, and loneliness. You hit the bottom, now what? You call on the Lord and keep moving.

Mr. Dorsey came to my parents' church when I was about five years old. He wrote music and Negro spirituals. Everybody loved him. It was a wonderful time. People got together and let the spirit move freely. They laughed and they shouted and they thanked the Lord. It was charged-up time. There has always been some sort of religious involvement in my life, and the song "Precious Lord" is a part of my music life forever.

•

Geraldine Collins was the first black social worker that I met that really took a genuine interest in the black community.

We were living in the apartment. I was working and the kids were in day care. Unfortunately I got fired from the hospital and had to go back on AFDC. I was so depressed. I had hit the bottom again. The electric company came and cut the lights off. We owed two bills and we didn't have any money. We were living in an apartment where we had to pay utilities. We had no money. I remember being in this apartment on Studebaker Street, down the street from where Geraldine Collins lived. For two days we were in the pitch dark at night. I had to bathe the boys in chilled water. Finally I couldn't take it any more.

I went down the street and talked to Geraldine and within a matter of days, my life was back on track. I hoped one day that I would be able to do some of the things for people that she had done for me. I think I've been fortunate. Geraldine Collins was the one that listened to your hurts and pains and made them her own. When we were in the dark, she made sure there was light.

•

Something was still missing in my life. It wasn't furniture or anything material. It was a feeling of spirituality — a spiritual depth for all that I experienced. I used to think, "How do I pray, or how do I say thank you, Lord, for how well things are going right now?" Physically I was reaching my goals, but mentally and spiritually I was missing something. I had two children and I was concerned about who would take care of them if something happened to me. I wondered if something happened to them or me, would we go to heaven?

I had my family. My brother Jake was a role model to me. Jake was always there for me to cushion my falls. He had a lot of problems too. He was always there after my father or my mother had disciplined me about something that I had done. He would take me for a walk when I was pregnant and wasn't supposed to be out where people could see me. He would walk with me and make me laugh. He had struggles in his life, but he remains a steadfast role model for me and my sons. He is a wonderfully built weight lifter, very sensitive. He gives a tough handshake.

My parents gave me life, and my sister has been a driving force in my life. My sister Rosetta raised us all plus three kids of her own and kept house. Rosetta cared about me. She combed my hair when I was little and kept me clean.

I grew up in the Baptist church; it was okay, but I didn't feel like it was my place of worship. I felt that God is whoever you want God to be, whatever you want God to be. You just need that ability to sit where you are and talk to the Lord. My father used to say, "You go to the church you choose to go to, as long as you go to some church." I guess that stayed in my mind, too. Where should I go to church? I remember riding around with a friend talking because I was depressed.

I passed St. Augustine's parish. It was so strange because I hadn't been to St. Augustine's for years, but it was still exactly the same church as when I was running around the St. Peter Claver House. I stayed connected to St. A's through the community. I wasn't going to church, but I was in touch with its people and Father Piel.

St. Augustine's is a black Catholic church where it was okay to be Catholic and to say Hail Marys. I've come to love the Catholic church. I just love the spirituality I find there and in me. I love how you can sit quietly in the back pew. As a mixed up kid, I used to go in the back of different churches and say, "What's going to happen to me?"

When I was arrested and sent to Girls School, I was in the back of St. Augustine's church thinking, and when I walked outside I was arrested. I always felt it was okay to go to St. A's. I could just be who I was and who I was going to be. If you didn't dress the very best, you could go to St. A's. If you were not the very richest, you could go to St. A's. St. Augustine's welcomed black people no matter what. It was our church.

When I went back to St. Augustine's in the late seventies, I found there was an uneasiness inside me. I just didn't know what to do. I thought about sending Jason to a Catholic school when he was ready to go to kindergarten. After I talked to some friends I ended up putting him in a Catholic school.

This oriented me toward the Catholic church and its people. I met up with Father Piel again and talked with him about coming back to the church. I wanted to know if as a single mother I would be welcome. He assured me it would be okay to come back.

•

After I got up enough courage to go to the church itself, I just sat in the back. I didn't say anything. Still, people recognized me. I was okay with them. I rejoiced!

Father Piel was working in a different parish at this time. And Father Phil Corbett was getting ready to become the new pastor at St. Augustine's. As I was returning to St. A's, pastors were changing, so it seemed a time of transition for everyone.

Father Phil reminded me so much of Christ because he lived, prayed, and truly cared for the poor. I like to call him the godfather of black spirituality and evangelization. He came in and immediately started evangelizing black people. I believe he has the genuine spirit of Jesus Christ. He walks among the poor; he walks among those who are fighting and punching; he comes into the situation and he offers more than what you think you need sometimes. I'm sure that's what Jesus Christ did. Father Phil walks among the people who need it. I have come to respect the man. St. Augustine's parish was there for me when I was dragging along spiritually.

St. Augustine's parish is something I just have to tell the world about, because you are not likely to run into its spirit in a typical suburban parish. It is a haven for a beautiful spirituality. It was a place where I felt like I belonged. It is home for all. All nationalities, all races somehow come together under a common name, a common ground, our Lord, Jesus Christ.

We come together to sing and to praise the Lord. We care about you — we don't care what color you are, we don't care about any of those things. We just want to make you feel at home. It doesn't matter what you need. If someone in St. Augustine's is hurting, we band together and bring out the true meaning of being a Christian.

I felt comfortable going there and saying, "I want to believe you. I want to worship you. I want to be one of your children. What I'm saying down here on the earth is just not holding me so strong to you. I need some faith. I need to know that you care and that you're seeing all the injustices, and that you're doing something about them."

This is what I needed to say. Going to St. A's during a time of quiet, you could say those things because you knew right around you there was someone that was thinking the same thing or feeling the same thing.

At St. A's I met the finest black Americans that you could ever know. They were role models for those of us who were struggling within the Catholic church. Fine families, like the Huddlesons and the Sudburys, had lived through the struggles of being a black and Catholic. They hung in there and they paved the way for those of us who are struggling behind them.

•

It was 1979, and it was a special year because it was the year that Father Phil baptized my boys. I was giving them to the Lord. I didn't know what I could do as a human to keep them on the right track. But I knew for a fact that if I turned their spirits and them over to the Lord in baptism that he would take care of them.

My kids! My kids are definitely the top. They're my best friends. I can talk to them about anything. They can talk to me about anything — except girls. They're ready to be manly and loving. I can't believe that they're ready to be madly in love. They have taken me, and tolerated me, and they're there with me. I know they think, "My God, the woman is mad." But we're friends. We want honesty, compassion, we want love and understanding. We love each other and it's great.

Soon after their baptism, I began to teach them about the Catholic church. I've always read stories to them. We'd talk about the saints. They were mostly white saints, but that's okay. We got through it. With some research in black Catholicism now I'm getting an opportunity to tell them about saints who are black. I felt so full and so satisfied after I baptized my kids. I thought that it was so important that they know there is a better day, and there is someone greater than all of us who looks over us. I trust God to know how to do things. So I want my children to know this too.

•

I'm a musical person and I was drawn to the musical spirit at St. Augustine's. That's where I bloomed, in St. A's choir.

I always wanted to know, "What can I give these people? I'm not anybody special. I'm a mother struggling in the church." But I just wanted to be a part of it. We've got the really rich, and we've got really upper class. And we've got all these regular people. And everyone is coming together under a common bond and they're saying, "Sing it!" The choir has backed me up many times.

The choir offered me a chance to share my gift — to sing a song! All the things that hurt me or have bothered me come out in song. The different pains make the song so mellow, so strong, and people feel it. After the song is finished, I feel better, and I figure this is my gift because of what I feel. I can bring it out well until people can't help but feel it too.

I had had so much pain in my life and spiritually I was drained. I had no one to talk to and things were just not well. I remember coming into St. Augustine's and joining the choir. Bob Huddleston, who was singing in the choir, and others asked me to sing.

At Thanksgiving someone gives a solo. It was the first time I sang "Precious Lord" at St. Augustine's. It was amazing. It was so peaceful. I looked around and there was not a dry eye in the place. It freaked me out.

I stood in front of the St. Augustine's community and sang "Precious Lord." When you sing "Precious Lord" you sing it with all your heart and soul and just give it your best. That's what I did and it was probably the most memorable time in St. A's. The response of the people was so wonderful. That song was amazing. People were feeling so good when they left. When I think of St. Augustine's and I think of music that I've done, I'm sure that singing "Precious Lord" at St. A's was one of the finest hours I've ever had. The community received me and I was a part of it. The Thanksgiving solo has been a tradition within St. A's for years, and I'm happy to have been a part of that tradition.

That spirit of song — it can't be beat. The spirit of song is a gift that God gave to me, and God told me to use it. I do, I use it to the best of my ability. I wouldn't be here without choir members and my friend Willa, who has played for me and supported me for years.

The boys and I became regular church goers. I could not wait to go to church because it was a time that we shared. I lived across the street from the Dillons, who were members of St. Augustine's, and we became friends. A lot of people who have become part of my life are also a part of St. Augustine's. No one could make me do it. They could lead me to it and say this is for you to do. I had to do it. The community of St. Augustine's offers so much.

•

It meant so much to Mr. Dorsey to put those words on paper and to say that he was feeling like he was losing it. That's the way I felt before I ran into St. Augustine's parish, before I eased my way back into its heart.

I often wonder how many times people walk past St. Augustine's and say, "How do I get in?" I rode past there and I thought to myself, "How do I go back to church? What do I do? Will people look at me funny when I come

in? Will they welcome me? Will I feel out of place? What
should I do?" How many times that thought crossed my
mind. Finally, the only thing for me to do was to go in.
I finally got the guts to go in. I figured many people ride
past who don't have a church or a home, who don't have
anywhere to go and want to know, "How do I get in?"
Just walk in.

Father Phil empowered black people to be themselves.
He took them to workshops and offered them opportunities
to be more involved in the Catholic church. It was such a
humble and learning experience for me to see the rectory
run by black people and see them taking care of a black
parish. The church was there for me to go to, to worship
with people that I know, and I know that they really care
about me. It's just too much. I was so lucky to run into
these people.

The parish was a teacher for me. It taught me so much,
and taught me on my own turf. The St. Peter Claver Fund
would feed you before the soup kitchen came. You could
come in and get a sandwich, get a word of good cheer. You
would know that even though you were tired and weak,
even though you were worn, somebody cared about you.
You just have to let them know how it hurts. You've got to
let them know how you feel. You've got to tell somebody.
If you tell it to the Lord, he'll lead you to the people, to
the place you need to tell them, to the person that you
need to tell it to.

I remember the song and I listen to how the words say,

> *Through the storms, through the night,*
> *Lead me on to the light.*
> *Take my hand, Precious Lord, lead me on.*

And I think of how stormy people's lives are. You have to
have somebody you can trust. You need to have a church.

You don't necessarily need a priest; you just need to have a church.

Don't give up. I think about the song and the words and how everybody usually has a time in their lives when they just can't take it any more and they want to do something really spacey or really crazy. But it's always important just to share with someone. It's good to release it in prayer, but it's also good to say it to someone that you trust and get another opinion. You need someone else to bounce it off of. St. Augustine's, through my storms and through the night, is one place. The people were there for me, and I'm grateful.

Chapter 4

HE TOUCHED ME

He touched me,
The joy that floods my soul.
Something happened and now I know
He touched me and made me whole.

Jesus comes to us as the stranger and the friend. I know him as my friends who have been there for me.

•

My life did begin to pick up. I was going to St. Augustine's and singing and feeling really good about things. I needed to move from the Studebaker apartment. We needed more room with the boys growing. I went to see Geraldine Collins, the community outreach worker, and the Holy Cross Justice and Peace Center to get the extra money I needed.

I first spotted Sister Susan Kintzele at St. A's. Even though I was in St. Augustine's feeling good, the right person just hadn't come around. I remember so plainly seeing Sister, but she had a really stern look on her face and deep, dark eyes and thick brows. Our eyes locked as I was singing a song. She didn't smile, she didn't have any

46

kind of reaction, but I knew that she was feeling something from the song.

I was okay with having the kids baptized, but there was something inside of me that kept nagging at me. I wasn't sure what it was, but it kept saying, "There's still more to be done, MayLee."

I wasn't sure how to go about it. I went to the rectory, and I talked to Father Phil Corbett. He suggested that I go to talk with Sister Susan, who was working at the Justice and Peace Center.

Somehow I got myself to Chapin Street to the Justice and Peace Center. I went in to talk with Susan, and I was welcomed. I needed someone to talk to, and I needed some direction and some guidance.

She offered me a chance to come down to the Center and volunteer some time. Somehow she saw something in me, something that I didn't see. It was hard for me to respond to her because I was so used to not trusting people. I was used to using them to satisfy my own personal need. I guess I thought I would be doing that to Susan. She wanted me to be honest with her. I wasn't sure how to do it. It was a long, hard struggle to establish a trusting relationship.

Sister Susan is a small, quiet woman. The two of us made a strange combination. Here I was, boisterous, loud, pushy, talking with this stern person who was saying to me, "What can we do to help you? What are some of the things you'd like to do? Let's talk about it." Through Sister Susan and her tender and firm guidance, I began to seek and to understand what was holding me back from being able to do anything. I think that I was insecure and frightened.

In the process of looking for somebody, I found Susan. It took a while for me to realize that she would be my friend and accept it. Many things were to cross my path before I actually became a trusted friend of Susan's and the Justice and Peace Center.

•

I came to know a very kind woman in St. Augustine's. Her name was Marge. One of her sons was baptized at the same time that Jason and Jaron were baptized. We became friends. Marge was just wonderful to me. We didn't lack for anything. She bought food for me when we ran out, she kept Jaron after school for me when he went to school for half a day so I could continue to work. She picked him up early on cold winter mornings and took him to school.

I began to depend on Marge and rely on her. Maybe I even took her for granted. But as I look upon it, it wasn't that I meant to take her for granted. I just got taken up with it, overwhelmed with it. I didn't mean to become greedy, but I guess I became overbearing and I demanded more of her than she could give at that time. Her own family began to suffer.

Sister Susan explained to me that you just can't take, take, take without people expecting something in return. But by then it was too late because Marge had become upset with me and depressed with me for not being the type of person that she thought I could be.

•

I was looking for a job. I was afraid to test myself to see if I could get the job. I was afraid I wouldn't fit. Sister Susan just looked at me and said, "Well, if you won't do it, then don't." She was quiet but steadfastly behind me. I can remember her being so small and so timid. I was bigger and rougher and I jumped up in front of her and said,

"Who do you think you are? I'll do...." I can remember her just standing in front of me and saying, "You'll do what?" This woman's not afraid of me. Let me get out of here. I knew then that she was tough, even though she was small.

With her quiet perseverance and presence, I was able to go to Father Corbett and sit down and get the job as Director of St. Peter Claver Emergency Assistance Fund. Strange as it seems, St. Peter Claver is the name of the house where I used to hang out as a kid. Now I had two kids, life went on, and I was coming back in the direction of the Catholic church. I was working my way back into it.

I got the job, because someone said, "Go down there and try." Also, the job required that I be working toward something. That's when I thought about school at Indiana University at South Bend (IUSB).

Susan would always come to me and explain things. Whether I was her mission, or whether she saw something in me that I didn't see in myself, I don't know. She would get mad and yell at me. She suggested that I not rely so heavily on people. I should rely on myself.

I registered and was accepted on probation. I was seeking a new beginning for myself. Little did I know that it would be so difficult — but not impossible. My life had begun to pick up. Jaron was in kindergarten and Jason in first grade. I was working part time at St. Augustine's and going to school full time.

Doors were beginning to open. My eyes were beginning to open. I was beginning to see that it was going to take work. There was no way that I was going to slide through life easily.

I had a determination and a drive that I didn't even understand. I had to learn what to say and what not to say — not to act so irrationally. I had to learn to slow

myself down. Most of all I had to learn to listen. If you
are on your own as long as I'd been on my own, you don't
listen to anyone. That was one of the hardest things for
me to learn, to listen to others.

I found that if you were not a good student in grade
school, college could be very difficult. I was not a good
student. From fifth grade on, I had a hard time being a
student. So college was doubly hard for me. I remember
plainly going to classes and writing papers in a beginning
English class. I got so many F's in that class! I was ready
to quit because I was upset that the teachers were mean
and hard. I figured that they didn't like me as a person,
and they were giving me F's to prove it.

I also thought they were prejudiced. I had all kinds
of excuses made up as to why I couldn't do it. But when
I tried a little harder, my papers got better. I needed
to sincerely make the commitment and really see myself
through it no matter what. I had a hard time holding on
to that commitment because I kept wanting to quit. I kept
trying, and what I was finding was so hard to swallow. I
had to work; I had to study every spare minute and more;
I had to take care of the kids.

But there was a drive in me. The drive came with that
English class — I don't care how many F's you give me,
eventually you're going to have to give me an A. Well, it
didn't work out like that. Eventually, I got a D to a C,
and a C to a B, but I can't say I ever got an A in English
031.

Trying new things is never a breeze. The best part,
though, is trying. God, I tried so hard. But sometimes I
didn't. When I didn't try, the grades I got reflected that.
Being a passing student meant that you had to maintain
a 2.0 average, which was a C. I fell below that a couple
of times. The next semester I would work harder to get
my average up. As soon as I had mastered one thing,

there was something new. Being a student was a constant learning experience.

•

I was also learning new personalities, learning new people, and learning from each of those people in a different kind of way. I learned that I was not the only person in the world that had suffered through something. I learned that no one's life is perfect.

Most people don't just sit back on their duff and wait for something to come and lift them out, lift them up. That's what I felt like before I began to try and trust in friends. I just kept blaming it on the Lord. "Lord, why are you treating me like this? Lord, don't you care that I'm hurting like this? Lord, don't you see that I'm poor? Lord, don't you see that I need this, Don't you see that I need that?"

Going to IUSB was the test of my life. The books so challenged me that I was often afraid of them. But today I do have a degree, which means that I hung in there. But it wasn't easy. I'd work at St. Augustine's and go to classes all day, then I'd come home to type my book reports. It would be after 11:00 p.m. I can remember not going to bed until after 4:00 a.m. and Susan waking me up at 6:30 a.m. in time to get the kids going. It's a degree well earned. They have my blood, sweat, and tears. It was a test of my person. IUSB was a challenge.

I began to think, "No wonder the Lord is not giving me all the blessings that I'm asking for. If he gave them all to me, I wouldn't do anything." I learned that not everyone is sympathetic to a sob story. They're sympathetic to a degree, but then they begin to think you've got to do something. You can become lazy by it all.

I had different teachers, compassionate teachers, teachers who didn't care, classes that were hard, classes that were easy. I was challenged all the time to be the best I could be. I had to learn to survive the lifestyle that I was living, being a mother, a student, and working to support my family. It was overwhelming at times. But each time I would learn something from someone new.

Another person I met at the Justice and Peace Center was Rita Kopcznski. Rita is in some ways like me. We both have strong personalities. There was always a kind of mutual respect. What Rita did and what she was for me was the person who offered little sympathy. It was hard for her too, so she wasn't about to let me get away with anything. She would say things to me that would shock me and make me angry, but I could sit back and see what she was trying to tell me. It was really hard for me to understand Rita and become a friend of hers. I would always tell her that I cared, and I knew she did. She always kept my mind challenged, she kept my mind moving. Rita showed me the world. She showed me new places.

I learned if someone constantly gives to you or helps you, then you begin to lose your drive. You need to work for it. Let me tell you, I remember staying up nights and crying because I didn't understand a word — instead of getting a dictionary and looking it up. "Poor MayLee. This is too hard for her. Nobody cares about her. She needs someone to care about her. She needs someone to tell her it's okay. She needs someone to say, 'MayLee you can do it.'"

Not until I began to believe I could do it was I able to accomplish anything. Then I had to stop and say, "Okay, you're looking for something. What are your looking for? A four-year degree. What kind of four-year degree? Sociology, Liberal Arts, something." I had to start setting goals.

I had many friends help me through this time in my life. Like Thomas Crowley. Tom Crowley, you can't beat him — an unselfish, rich businessman who is so human. He and his wife adopted four biracial children on top of their two natural children, two girls and two boys. He is unique. He took care of his girls and boys and he took us, Jason, Jaron, and myself, under his wing. He offered us love and financial backing. He was rich, but not in money only. Tom was a class-A act. He gave lectures; he went around town; he gave me tapes on asserting myself. He told me to listen to the tapes one by one to get the motivation I needed. He brought food, tapes, encouragement, and taught me to drive. He sent me to driving school. I had never driven a car until two years ago. It was the best!

If you're looking for nothing, you're going to find nothing. It took me a while to see that. Above all it's through people like Susan who would say to me in a certain way, "If you want it, you have to work for it. I can help you understand it, but you have to write it." Or a person like Rita who challenges me or a Tom Crowley saying, "You're as smart as you want to be." Inside my mind I was saying, "You're no fool. Of course I know that I can do this." Part of me wants to be lazy and think that I can't. It took me a long time to believe that I could.

•

I looked for many ways of self-improvement. Sometimes I took it too far. I tried to change who I was — I tried to be somebody else. It didn't work because of the incredible amount of phoniness. I would try to prove that I was an intellectual by looking up words, and then I would fall on my face by using them in the wrong context in a sentence. Rita would say, "No, that's not the way to do it. You're acting like some kind of fool." I'd get so mad at her.

"How dare you say I'm acting like a fool! I'm trying to find myself!"

I moved along in my schooling. I thought the longer you go, the better school gets. I just went right through. I didn't take a semester off, I didn't take a break, I went every winter and fall. I began to listen more to what people said, and I began to work with Susan and Rita and the other people at the Justice and Peace Center. And they offered me opportunities that I would never have had a chance to be a part of without them.

The Holy Cross Justice and Peace Center (really Rita and Sister Susan) invited me to a conference in Deer Park, Maryland, where I met Joe Holland. I found a friend in Joe. I recently discovered that he is very famous, but none of that touches the guy I know — the family man. No one superextraordinary, but a caring human being. The world needs more people like Joe.

At Deer Park, Joe was talking about social justice. I didn't understand a word he said. I really felt left out because I really wanted to know. He seemed to know his stuff and I was looking for something to motivate me, to make me feel more a part of the Catholic church, more than just coming and sitting and singing and leaving.

He had ideas about lay people — how we empower ourselves. I was turned on by that. The one thing that I respected most about this man was when I approached him and told him I didn't understand, he sat right down and said, "What didn't you understand?" And he explained it.

The people in my life exposed me to things wider than my own backyard. They helped me to look beyond my sadnesses and my weaknesses. They helped me through a terrible time in my life. They would hold me when I thought no one would. By right, I would get straightened out good when I needed it. I would get hurt and slam the door like a brat saying, "I'm going to take my marbles and go home." And they would just leave me. When I came back I would be a little more humble and seeking some more of their guidance.

Being with friends means that you will find something. There's no guarantee what you'll find, but there is something to be found. Telling someone that you need help won't always guarantee someone like Rita or Sister Susan, but I can guarantee that someone is listening. I'm convinced that you can't do it alone. You need a cushion to fall on.

Even if you hit the bottom, the bottom becomes a U. You go to the bottom, and you see what it's like down there. But you don't stay. You just come up in another direction. If you get an F on a paper, you go to the bottom and get all depressed about the F, at least I would, and then I would get another F because I was so depressed. Then I would talk to someone, and I would say, "I don't want another F. It's too hard to get them off your report card." So I studied harder. But I didn't learn that by myself. I learned it by bouncing it off someone else, someone who loves me.

Sister Susan Kintzele is independent and stern and has kept her eyes on the prize. I think about how she's always been there for me. Our differences are what attracted us and her strong will behind my constant perseverance was just an unbeatable combination. But to be her friend really wasn't easy. Sister's community was very protective, and they were very skeptical of Susan getting to know the likes of me. At that time, I was a very confused and troubled woman. But not confused enough to quit. I always had drive. I just needed some direction.

There were many doubts as to whether our friendship would last. Not just from her, but from my friends and my parents who couldn't believe that I was friends with a nun. Where we came from nuns and priests were up on a pedestal where you just didn't talk to them. You didn't even know if they were really human. I just saw the nuns walking around in long black dresses with paper plates on their heads. I didn't trust them a bit. I had nothing to say to them.

Sister gave the nun image a whole new perspective for me. She was a real person, dressed like a person, talked like a person, had the same problems as everybody else. It took me a long time to tell her the truth. She would always catch me in a lie. Then I discovered that it was easier to tell her the truth. If you told her a lie she would dissect it until she got down to the truth, so you might as well start off with the truth. With any friendship, there are conflicts. Any hard times aren't anything compared to friendship.

I needed self-confidence. That's what I got from Sister Susan. My open and outward personality was something that she needed because she is so quiet. We complemented each other very much. At one time, when you said "friend" to me, I didn't even know the meaning of the word. Now I know.

•

I think the strength of my friendship with Sister Susan lies in our differences. It's the differences that people possess that somehow complement each other. If we were all the same, no one could help anybody. I find strength in those who are similar too, like my friends Pearline, Marie, and Stephanie. You'd say, "I'm down, and you're down." But it's those that aren't down who can help you, if they will.

My friends have steadfastly helped me all around — the whole person. And they're people that you have to call by name. It's like a bird being pushed out of the nest. You push it once and it falls. You push it again and it begins to find its wings. Eventually, it can fly. Sister Susan and Rita helped me get my wings and fly. They have been there for me. We are a triangle that has been broken and split up, but it never loses its strength.

Be your own best friend, like yourself as much as other people do — I do like me. Sometimes I don't because I talk too much and I'm pushy, but I'm going to be honest and open. I'm going to be me. Me is what's calling people — not someone else or what I think someone else would like me to be.

If you have friends like I have, tell them you are thankful for them. Tell them how much you appreciate them and how much you love them. It's okay. I try to give my friends presents. I give them gifts, sometimes when they least expect it. Not when it's a holiday, but just something to say, "I care, I care." If they want to acknowledge it, it's okay. If not, I'm still their friend.

Christians should be used to struggles and hardships. No saint that I ever admired had it easy. They're always looking to find something or someone who will help them. That's what we have to do. We have to keep trying. We knock on one door and the door is slammed in our faces. We just have to keep looking because somewhere somebody loves you. Somewhere someone cares. Maybe it's not your parents or the people who raised you, but there is somebody for everybody. I believe that. There was somebody for me. Because of that I was able to continue my education, continue my learning process, and work to help other people. I was offered the chance with my job at St. Augustine's to open the door that people knocked on. I became the person that people sought out. I traded places. I wasn't the seeker, I was the person they were finding.

Friends are the hands of Jesus.

Shackled by a heavy burden
'Neath a load of guilt and shame,
Then the hand of Jesus touched me,
And now I am no longer the same.
He touched me and made me whole.

Chapter 5

THE LORD WILL MAKE
A WAY SOMEHOW

It's hard for me to refer to poor people and not think of myself. I realize that I have a lot to be thankful for. I've come a long way and I can look at poverty and see it for what it is. I have had to say that to myself many times as I worked at St. Augustine's and as I worked with the people I met at the Justice and Peace Center.

I had only to rely on faith. Faith that somehow no matter what I attempt to do or how I attempt to do it, I'm rewarded just for making the effort.

It's hard to go into community outreach work with no idea of what to expect. I went to work at St. Augustine's and people started coming to me with their problems. I was trying to do everything that I could. I worked for a priest who was really nice, but he was always holding a hand over me. I always felt like I never quite added up, and I wasn't always sure why I was there. After a period of time, I figured I would just do the very best that I could.

•

I wasn't really aware of what it meant to work. I didn't have a real good work record. Before, if I got tired, I'd quit. I wouldn't even write to say I was quitting. It's just a habit I got into. When I got tired of working as a nurse's aid or whatever, I just quit. As I've grown, I've learned what it means to work. To go to work every day, on time, and get everything done that you are expected to do. This is tough. It was hard to learn what it means to have a job.

When I opened the door to give money or food or whatever to people who need it, I ran into all kinds of people and problems. I had $300 of emergency funds each month to help. The first year that I was there was the hardest. People would get mad at me because I wouldn't give them what they wanted whenever they wanted it. I had to stand in a position of judging who gets this and who does not. Who's most deserving? Who's the poorest? Who's the most needy? That's really hard.

I would get so upset when someone came in and told me that they had three kids and they were starving to death and everything was gone. I would immediately write a food order to help them. I'd feel so good that I had helped someone. Then someone else would come and say, "My gas is about to be cut off." Then I'd write out a check and all the money would be gone. Then for the rest of the month, people would still be calling for help. I began to take a little more precaution.

There were days I couldn't eat or sleep because I was so worried and so shocked that people were worse off than me. I would sit around for days at my house and I would think, "Poor me. Poor MayLee. She doesn't have this or she doesn't have that." Then I would find out that there are people worse off.

•

I'd help a lot of people and then someone would say something rotten about me, like I didn't help them. There were days when it was a jungle. I didn't know what to do or say. I just kept thinking, "If I can just help two or three people who really need it, then I've done well. If I don't, I'm not any good. I'm not doing the job well." It was fortunate that I knew some people who worked in social services. Every time there was a question about a particular individual, I would call my friends on the phone, and I would ask if they knew the person I was dealing with and whether or not that person needed help.

I learned so much from the people — they're so humble. Some of them would do better if they could. I just don't know the answers. I didn't know the answers then, and I don't know them now. I just know that St. Augustine's church sponsored the direct assistance program for those in need.

The good things were that every Thanksgiving we gave baskets and every Christmas we gave toys. They probably weren't the best toys, but they were toys. To see the kids' eyes light up and to have the mothers thank you for these extra pieces of toys was humbling.

I was influenced so much by poor black women. That was my target group. I learned so much from them. There is a steadfastness about them. I noticed that even in myself.

We've been beaten, we've been hurt, we've been ridiculed, we've been taught all kinds of things. Of the many poor black women that I have served, there are some that are just treacherous and don't care what they do, but there are some of the most sensitive, most loving young mothers and old mothers who take care of their kids. I saw a lot of rotten ones and an awful lot of good black women coming through there.

I just think this is an opportunity for me to say thank you to those that were there for me and that helped me through it by being my friends and hearing me out. And also to thank the ones like Mary Keaton who made me a stronger and a more open person.

●

I was learning in the classroom and then coming and living in the real world with something else to learn. Being a parent I taught my kids that this is an open world and you can get what you want if you make it. Many times I felt like I couldn't because I was so overpowered by the poverty, so overpowered by the needs of people.

Another challenge for me was to be a mother and to be a good mother and a fit mother. I always promised myself that I would never hit my kids. I promised we would talk it over. I do backfire on that. Sometimes I would have to swat their butts. I have to let them know that they can't run me over. I have to struggle with being a mother because I started off being rotten as hell. I didn't know what was right. I was afraid of the challenge of having two kids by myself and having to make sure that they become well rounded people. It was hard but it became okay. We've fought, we've yelled, I've been threatened with all kinds of things, but we talk about it. We keep an open channel.

I found that motherhood is a series of events. The kids are happy and sad but there are seldom occasions that you see your kids as real people. Then all of a sudden you're having a serious conversation with them. I know the situation could have been better if I had a husband to help me out, but I'm thankful to God that they are as well as they are now.

I was moved by the black women in our community. When the women came to me with their stories, I could tell if it was the truth or a lie. If a woman came to the door and she was already crying, I knew that she was trying to get to me. But I figured that if anybody came to my door crying and in need of help, I had to give it to them.

I shared their pain — pain of men, pain of children growing out of control, and the pain of feeling tied down because of the depression you feel, the helplessness you feel. It's just incredible. There were nights that I went home and I couldn't eat. I'd think about this poor lady with six children who didn't have any place to stay, and I'd begin to pray. I'd say, "Look, Lord, I want to be of service to these women. But I need you to help me."

•

I faced many problems with the poor women who would come to see me. I would see their daughters who were just products of their mothers, and I would always feel compelled to tell them what I thought honestly and openly. If you came to the West Side of town and you said, "Could you tell me about MayLee?" most black people would tell you, "Yeah, I know her and she's so and so, but she'll help you." They knew that I was doing the very best that I could. I often needed strength and, as always, I drew my strength from a song. The song that brought me through it was "The Lord Will Make a Way Somehow."

I'm sure that God sees my suffering. I'd draw strength from my songs and my music. I'd just sit there and sing this song when I was so overburdened and did not have someone I could relate to. Eventually there were people that would come to St. Augustine's to get some help and would give me something in return. On the days that I was being incredibly unfriendly, they would say, "MayLee, what's wrong?" I'd say, "You know, I have these problems, too." They would understand and give me encouragement to keep on going. I really loved the West Side women. They were my friends. I grew up with them. I lived with

them, and my struggles were their struggles too. There
was a mutual sharing. My admiration for black women is
just incredibly high.

I know the stereotypical picture of black women. They
are strong and tough. So why do they need help? Don't
get me wrong, I've met some strong and tough ones as
I've worked five years on the West Side of town. I believe
that any woman who works now is strong and tough —
particularly the black women. They are incredible. They
just won't quit, even when they're beaten and they've got
two black eyes. The things that you'll take just to have
someone love you. I feel that in myself sometimes. I told
them they should leave him, quit him, forget him, but
I knew it took more than talk so I offered my love and
support.

I began to share with the black women who would
listen that there is another way. We'd go to Geraldine
Collins's house and have talks in her living room. We
supported each other. Through it all we seemed to say:
"I'm getting older, I'm not getting any better, I'll have to
settle."

We talked all the time about "not settling." Just not
settling for anything and looking for something better. I
would have to pray really hard because many would not
listen to me. They would simply do what they felt like.
But if I talked to ten women that week, one or two of them
would take something that I told them and use it in some
way. They would do something to change their life. I felt
I was making a small dent in their deep walls of pain.

•

That's when I felt like I was doing some good, like I was
doing a service to people. That's just one group of people
that I worked with.

I met another group of people at the Justice and Peace Center — the intellectuals who are very much in tune with the needs of the whole world. I sometimes felt caught in the middle of the two groups. I always felt like I was somewhere in between — a group of white, educated, nice women who represented the wider and white church community, and my own black community, the women that I grew up with who were so different.

I felt as though I were caught in a tug-of-war. I needed to be aware of my roots and my friends that I've grown with. I also needed to talk to this other group who challenged me intellectually. The women who I've known for years challenged me too. But it was beginning to seem that they only wanted me when I had money or some way of helping them.

When I decided this was not the help they needed, I became Uncle Tom, kissing up. That began to bother me. The problem was, "Where do I fit, where do I belong, who am I, who do I want to please, why do I want to please them?" I'd tell the women, "I'm your friend, I'm your friend, I'm not changing. I'm just trying to do better." Then I'd run over to my white friends and say, "What's wrong with me? Can you help me? Tell me what to do." It was really a vicious time. I'm so close to the root of it all.

This is where I begin to think that there really is a separation in our worlds. I believe that it's an equal world and we can share the territory. At one time in my life I felt like I was never going to get out. I'd go to school and read about the oppressed, I'd go home and work with the oppressed, and then I'd have to write a paper on the oppressed. I was living in two different worlds with different ideas, and I wasn't sure what to do.

This is where that person who's your friend, who you care most about, comes in. This is where a sounding board is needed — someone who can listen and who you can talk to about your problems. In my case it was Sister Susan. She would say, "Okay, MayLee, what are we going to do about it? So we can move on to the next thing?" She was that constant sounding board for me. "Yes, we see this and it's bad, but what can we do about it right now?" I was able to do something about it, so I continued to do my work.

That's why I think it's so important that our differences are preserved. When another person looks at the same situation differently you gain a new perspective for yourself. It's so important; we need that. I always needed the side of me that challenges ideas as much as the side of me that continues to struggle with my people. That's why I think that it's important that we share our gifts among each other freely, openly, nothing artificial, nothing phony. Just be ourselves.

●

As I look at my life's journey, there has always been an inner faith in me that could get me to go the extra mile. When I would come home with all these things pressing on my mind I'd want so much to be the very best person that I could be.

I would see people getting killed, I would see people getting hurt, I would see girls getting beat up, I would see a constant flow of pregnancies, I would see unhappy black women every day, and it was beginning to make me feel like I couldn't make it. But someone has been there pushing me.

It's so easy to slip. Living and working and being among the poor people every day takes its toll. The song that reminds me of this part of my journey tells me, "the Lord will make a way somehow." The words go,

Like a ship that's tossed and driven,
Battled by the angry sea,
When the storms of life are raging
And the fury falls on me,
I wonder what have I done
That makes this race so hard to run,
But I said to my soul,
Don't worry, for the Lord will make a way somehow.

I would remember the words, and I would hum this song. Somehow I could keep going. I really believe that working and praying and death and resurrection continue the flow of life. We just get over them as they come, working with the people and learning not to carry every problem on our shoulders and learning to be able to separate ourselves from the problems. For me it took a lot of work and a lot of prayers.

After I got home one night after an angry outburst at the Justice and Peace Center, I went to my room. I was kicking things around the room and the Bible fell on the floor. It was so strange because I went to pick it up and I was still all huffy and mad yet I began to read. It said,

> For his anger is but a moment,
> and his favor is for a lifetime.
> Weeping may tarry for the night,
> but joy comes in the morning.

I thought, "Why is that there?" I could not make the connection. How does this fit into my life? I wrote it down in my journal.

As I reflect now, it's true — joy comes in the morning, no matter how rotten things are. I had a dream that I had an opportunity to work with my people, poor people, and then to go to school and get a degree and get a job. This plays in my mind all the time.

•

I learned that I couldn't change the whole black population of the West Side even though I wished I could. I could only do what I could do. Over the years as I worked I mellowed and I helped as many as I could help with what I had. I was thankful to God for that, for the chance to have a little money to help those who were truly needy. I was trying to meet their needs and the needs I had by doing something for my people.

It was a time when I really believed in the Lord. I never had a doubt. The Catholic church offered its money, support, and prayers, and the people came with open hearts and listened to what I had to say after I gave the money. I always felt that if I was going to give them $20 I could give them a lecture, but I would always try to be tactful. I'd say, "Let's reach for something better. Register to vote." I would talk and talk over and over and I would think that I wasn't doing any good. But now I'm sure that it was good.

I love the church. It has its faults, but it has always brought me such security. It always brought me a priest who I could totally trust and I could tell whatever I wanted to, although it wasn't always in language that he could understand. But everyone that I ever turned to has always accepted me.

•

"The Lord will make a way." As I approached the end of my senior year, I just quit working. I remember a priest friend of mine saying, "Don't graduate before you gradu-

ate." Someone would always bring me back. That's why
I'm convinced that the Lord will make a way for us, but
we have to make a way for us too in the sense that we help
each other.

We'd like to change the world, and I'm working at doing that. You can't do it alone. You have to go it alone
sometimes, but not always. It's good to have different people who see things differently. I come to see what they're
thinking, and I know what I'm thinking so that two parts
make a perfect fit. That's what I always say about the
team effort that I've experienced.

The spirit of God tells us that it doesn't matter how
heavy the burden is or how long you have to carry it, God
will make the way for you. You just have to believe that
even though good fortune passed you by and even though
it seems that you are never going to get it, it's a test of
faith. "Can you hold out? Lord, help me to hold out. Yes,
I can hold out. "

•

Even after I found friends, my work wasn't over. There is
still a lot to be done and a lot that I have to take. At the
time, I wasn't making any money. I was depressed because
I was trying to help everybody I could on the West Side
and I was going to school and buying books and trying
to make Jason and Jaron happy. All these opportunities
would be mine if I could just hold out and make it through
till the end.

It was a scary journey. I started out at the bottom
of the totem pole. It seems that's where they start black
women. You have to work your way up. I worked the job
for years doing whatever was needed: food, money, rides,
whatever I could do. Then I had to go to classes in the
morning and classes in the evening. Then I'd come home

in the evening and be a mother, check homework and say this is wrong and this is right, hug and kiss my kids to let them know that I loved them, put them to bed, study half the night. I kept saying, "This is too hard. I can't do it." Then I'd hear, "If you can't do this, what are the alternatives?" I rode on hope and prayers. You hope and pray. And you say, "Joy is coming in the morning, joy is coming."

You just have to hang in there and take the falls and take the down moments. Everybody has down moments. But I've had moments that I was so down that I thought the world was just going to cave in on me. Then you hear, "Let's go out, let's pull away, let's look at it from another direction."

No matter how rough it is, you just have to keep persevering. I keep thinking of the part of my journey where I began to question, "Who am I? Who do I want to be? Do I want to be a social worker, do I want to be this?" It's a question period within yourself. Then you break down and you cry and cry and think that you can't make it anymore. Then that voice echos in the back of your mind, "This is a test of your faith, MayLee. Because the going is tough and time is hard, will you break? Will you give it up for me? Will you just quit and go back to the life you hated?"

No, you don't. You just trust in the Lord and know that he makes a way. It's been proven. In the darkest moments, there is always a flicker of sunshine, a flicker of light.

•

I'm writing about my journey from the bottom up. I came into this from the bottom with you. I was not expected to succeed, but some did think I could succeed.

How far can I go? Can I really make it through? Can I make it through in time? Will I last through this? Will I feel empty like this forever? Does anybody appreciate the fact that I'm out here trying to help my people, trying to help the young mothers learn about themselves, how to teach them to say, "No," taking care of the senior citizens.

All this is part of the job I had. Taking care of the senior citizens. Making sure that their needs were met. People died around me all the time. I buried people, helped people to know that there is a better life, tried to show them a way out.

I had two friends that were locked up in prison. I used to write them all the time and tried to show them that someone cared. It's me, I only have $5 or $10 to send you, but you could use it. I'd always get a note back saying, "MayLee, thank you, girl. We love you."

I'd think to myself, it's the little things. That wasn't a hard thing for me to do, it was pretty easy. I just loved the idea of having people live the best they could. You just have to try. Nothing is going to happen if you just sit there making nothing happen.

I began to feel that somebody was listening to me. Not everyone was listening to me, but certainly the young girls and the kids were beginning to listen to me. I could tell by the fact that they'd come to the rectory and sit down and see if there was a job I needed to get done. Then I would find out what was really going on in them and what they really needed most. I was just trying to be their friend.

Chapter 6

ONE DAY AT A TIME, SWEET JESUS

I was trying to do too many things. That's when I had to back up and try to search out me. What is it like being me? Finding myself and taking me to the heights.

> *One day at a time,*
> *That's all I'm asking of you.*
> *Give me the strength to do*
> *All the things that you want me to do.*

It was a time in my life when I felt like I was going to have a nervous breakdown. I felt like quitting everything. Even with what everyone else had said, I felt like, "This is it. I can't do it any more, I'm going to quit."

It's very easy to let my life get out of control. I guess when I think of "One Day at a Time" I realize that my life was beginning to get out of control. I was working, I was a mother, I was in college and studying, I was doing emergency assistance for the poor.

There were days when I couldn't even go the grocery store because people knew me, and they would come up to me and say, "MayLee, when can I come over and get some help?" So I could never really shut my job down as director at St. Peter Claver Emergency Assistance. People felt very comfortable approaching me — at the store, in the mall, anywhere — to tell me their problems.

I began to think, "Gee, people really have a lot of confidence in me." But then I also realized that people were beginning to use me and to take my kindness as a weakness. I would have people knocking on my door late hours of the night.

The time that I most panicked was the day that a young girl had come down from Gary with her boyfriend and was going to live with him. She found out that the boyfriend had a wife and he brought this young girl to his house and his wife was out of town. His wife came home early and he just put this young girl out on the street. She had two kids. They appeared at my door. The baby was wet and she was crying. She said, "MayLee, I lived in Gary and I came down here with this dude." That was one of my first problems that I tackled as Director of St. Peter Claver Assistance Fund. I let her come into the rectory and she washed up and gave the kids a bath. I sent her home to her mother.

One night there was a young girl that came knocking at my door about 2:00 or 3:00 a.m. I didn't even know who she was, but there she was with two little babies. She said, "Are you MayLee Johnson? Someone told me that you live here, and I need a place to stay. I came here with my boyfriend, and he left me." And I had to let her in. Then I would end up being responsible for that person until she found a home. It was beginning to have an affect on me.

A friend of mine was shot and he was bleeding. The police were after him. I had to decide what to do. I told him to go to jail so they could fix him. He got better and he came into the outreach program at St. Augustine's hurt

and in trouble again. I called the police and the ambulance
and they took him to the hospital. The second time he
wasn't so lucky. He got shot in the back and was paralyzed.
He eventually died. My most humbling experience with
him was talking to him about turning himself in. Then
watching how the cops treated him, I almost felt bad that
I had turned him in.

•

In my senior year at IUSB, I was failing some classes.
There were lots of drugs where we lived on Colfax, and
there came a point — a real decision point in life. I was
running around, I was going to school, and my own son
was getting away from me.

One day they were out in the back playing, and Jaron
came in and said, "Momma, Jason and Tony are in the
back, and they're going to smoke a joint." I thought, "My
God, are they really going to smoke a joint?" I had to sit
for a few minutes and think, "My God, my life is out of
control. My kid is ten years old and he's about to experience drugs. What do I do?"

Being the person I am with faith that the Lord is with
me and just knowing that if you are honest and you do
your best, things will come out as best they can, I decided
to approach him. I called him in and they dropped the
joint outside. I had to turn the porch light on to find it. I
picked it up off the ground and brought it into the house.
Jason and Tony were before me.

I wasn't sure what to do, so I told them they could
smoke it. I told them to fire it up right now in front of
me, and I didn't want them sneaking behind houses trying
to do it. If they had to try drugs, I wanted them to be
in a safe place with someone who could rush them to the
hospital. They were too shocked to continue. I told them

I was having some problems myself, but I didn't feel like I needed to get high.

After this, I felt like I needed to come to some kind of grip with my life. Was my life out of control? The incident with Jason was the straw that broke the camel's back. I saw my own son messing around with drugs. I found out that after we talked about it, they decided they didn't want to smoke. We talked about what it meant for me to be going through school. It might have seemed to them like they were being neglected, but they had to know that I loved them. They assured me of their love.

Things were progressively getting worse. Nothing was coming together. I had been so sure that my last year would be the easiest. I am now convinced that we must take it one day at a time, one step at a time.

It's really great to have someone that you trust and that supports you to back you so when things are really rotten, you can go and say, "This is how I feel. Can you talk with me?" One of the biggest problems is the lack of communication and the lack of trust between people. Especially as a black woman, I find it extremely hard to go to a "regular" person and say, "I feel like this." It took me years and years to trust people. It's been a long time. Now I can trust a few people, and I can bounce it off a few people and say, "What do you think?"

•

I was considering myself truly poor. The street life is outrageous. I'm not sure that Middle America realizes how hard it really is for poor America to get through. People suffer so much here and they suffer because of the lack of things — lack of education, lack of motivation.

I think God calls me to be there as a motivator for those who are not motivated. I've seen to what extent I could be effective with helping people. It took a long time for me to work my way through that. I can't help every poor black woman who comes through the door. I can't help every poor child who comes to the door.

When I first went to work, I wanted to do that. I thought that I was Christ. From everything that I've read, and everything that I could see about Jesus, he was constantly in touch with the poor people. Never giving them just money and blessings, but doing whatever he could at the time that it was needed and then walking away from it. He would not sit there and say, "Come here and check out this miracle I worked." He worked his miracles and he continued to go about the country and tell people of the good news of the Lord.

There was no way that I could help every poor person that needed something from me, but I felt that I was a failure if I didn't. I felt that this was what I was called to do. Helping people in pain was also just listening and not passing judgment.

Every day I learn something and every day I grow a little more. I refuse to go backwards. There's a whole world out there waiting for someone to tap into it. I'm convinced it's not going to be easy for blacks, but I'm convinced that we've been making steady strides for two hundred years.

●

I believe that this is the year for me. Nothing has really given me that idea, but I still take the same approach. If I could just get the strength that I need to get through the things that I must get through. I can't worry about everything around me. I can only worry about what I need to do and getting it done, what my job is at that particular time, what my role as a mother is, and what my role as myself is. It was not easy to become the person that I'm becoming.

I try to be able to say, okay, there's just so much that I can do. I still have problems with that. There are days when I cry because I'm convinced that I can't take the pressure. I'm convinced that there will always be some kind of pressure, and you have to begin to think that you can handle it.

I'll never forget my friend Marva, who's a member of St. Augustine's parish. She was having many problems at the same time. She was a strong support for me because she had already been through college. My problems and hers stemmed back to when we were twelve years old. There has always been a really good connection between us. It was strange because it was one of the Sundays when I was considering saying the hell with it, I'm going to quit school.

At just the point where I felt like giving up, Marva said to me that I looked tired and depressed. I said, "Well, I just feel like quitting." Then she told me that she was going to sing this song for me and it would help me. She went to the front of the church and said to everyone, "I'm going to sing this song for MayLee. I hope that it makes her feel better." The name of the song was "One Day at a Time." I was so moved.

As I listened to her sing "One Day at a Time," I was taken. I didn't know what to do, so I cried. I thought that I would have to sing that song some day. I'm influenced so much by music that people sing. I listen to different singers and different types of music. Then I think, "What song tells about this journey that I'm on? What song would take me through?"

It was "One Day at a Time." Things were really rough and it wasn't looking any better. To simply hear the words sung, it became part of me. I was rekindled somehow.

"I've got to make this journey, and I've got to take it one day at a time."

That's basically how I still do it. I was doing it at that time. No matter how rotten it is, I'm just trusting in this one day. If I get through it, I'm sure that tomorrow will take care of itself.

●

Life has a fast pace. The best thing that we can really do is just take it easy. If you get too busy, or have too many irons in the fire, you can't do anything effectively. What we need is thorough and effective things, and not quick, fast things.

Jesus loves us, he loves me. I have no doubt of that. I love Jesus too. The things that have happened in my life have all been stepping stones to reaching love, the maximum of my person.

Life reminds me of a U, where you go all the way to the bottom. The bottom isn't a pit, but kind of a turn that turns you back up. Each time you go to the bottom it's okay, because it's like a sliding board that goes up and down. As soon as you hit the bottom, it's not the pits forever. You can find another direction to come up.

That's where I'm at. I'm working on being the best that I can be. The person I am and the things I'm doing now are sufficient for the moment.

Chapter 7

I'VE COME TOO FAR

I draw strength from my faith and my friends. I want to free myself up from describing what my life was like and concentrate on my faith — the faith that I have relied on over the years. This faith is crucial. It is my spirituality!

From the time I was a little girl, I remember a picture of Jesus in our house. I remember so plainly that in the living room of our house there was this picture. If you turned your head one way it turned into the Lord's Supper and if you turned your head the other way the picture changed. I loved that picture.

But on that picture was a white man with a brown beard, and a long slender face, the typical Jesus picture. That was my first real perception of Jesus. For the longest time when we went to church I used to think that Jesus was the man in that picture.

•

As I continued to explore my religion and faith and what I wanted to believe in, I found the Catholic church was always there for me. It took a while to actually get in the church. I used to walk past churches and I'd think, "I wonder how I get in there. It's so big and beautiful."

These were the traditional churches in the South Bend area. So I figured, you just walk in. There's no big deal on how to get into the church.

As a young kid, I used to walk in the church and sit in the back pew. It's so ironic now because I'd sit there and think. I'd hide in the very back pew in St. Patrick's. The solitude, the quiet, the beautiful statues and pictures were my escape from the outside pressures that were so much a part of my life. Every time my life was struck with tragedies and unhappiness, someone has rescued me. The Catholic church has always been a haven for me.

It really didn't matter where the church was — in a black or white neighborhood — I would go in and sit down and pray. I always considered the church my safe place. As I got older and got in trouble and had no place to stay, I'd sneak into the church before they locked it up and stay there. I've slept in the back of them. I was discovered one morning in the back. "Okay, it's time to go now." Now I know why I found a blanket in the back pew.

Since that time, church has been a part of my life and growth. I always felt the spirit and the quiet. Just to sit down and talk to Jesus Christ and know he is my personal savior. I've hit rock bottom in my prayers but never in my faith. Faith is steadfast. There is hope for me. They told me a long time ago there was no hope for me. They told me, "You're doomed to be dead before you're fifteen." But I'm still here.

My faith is nurtured by St. Augustine's. The spirit is loud. Our black tradition in music and song and prayer is allowed to flow freely. So what if I'm not a member of a big fancy Catholic church. I can go to St. Augustine's and I can sing and get rid of all the tensions that I feel during the week. Just before I get ready to sing my song I hope that the song I am going to sing will truly touch somebody's heart, and that I can do my very best. If I ever hit the note the first time and it's right, it's right. That's part of your faith. Having a church community that supports and cares for you and congratulates you and appreciates you. That nurtures the faith that I have.

•

I feel that the church has problems. I really think it's too bad because they're just sitting back and letting golden opportunities ride by. For as long as I can, I'm going to battle those problems where it has to do with the laity and women and especially where it pertains to black Catholics.

I think it's very important that the Catholic church change and begin to accept people for their differences. We need to believe in each other a little bit more and support each other more. We must allow people to be different and accept their differences and learn from their differences and be enriched by their differences.

That's where the black church has a gift of rejoicing in music. No compromising or changing it back to the traditional — just jammin' and rejoicing and thanking God we're still here.

The way I feel as a black woman in the Catholic church is that wherever I am is cool. There's not a lot of women who have been there to lay any kind of pattern of how it should be.

The church has a long way to go but it's done a lot too. I think sometimes we're so busy beating up on the church that we don't take time to recognize the gifts that the church has given to minorities. The church has always been a learning institution for blacks. We could always get in. There have always been helping hands agencies around, like St. Augustine's and St. Peter Claver House. Catholic Charities has been here for years.

I would say that the church needs work, but I also say,

"Thank you." Thank you for a job well done. Thank you for the opportunity to let me study what it means to be a black Catholic. It means believing in the church and Christ and the Lord God above all. The church needs people of difference, and the church shouldn't be afraid to let these people walk in and share their gifts.

Its not just the European American Catholic church, it's the African American Catholic church, it's the Hispanic American Catholic church, it's the Asian American Catholic church, it's the Native American Catholic church, and it's one church for all. We're going toward it. It may not be in one year or five years or ten years, but a change is going to come. I hope I'll be around to see it and to be a part of it.

•

My spirituality has been nurtured by the opportunities I've had to pull away from it all and talk it over with my friends. I tell them, "This is how I've been feeling and I wonder if you can understand or if you can lend me an ear." So in my faith journey, in my growing to become a whole person and doing the things that are expected of me, in receiving so much, I begin to think that of those to whom much is given, much is expected. I continue to give as much as I possibly can to all around me. Then I pull back some for myself. I pull back a few minutes to take care of myself and to quiet myself.

I often take retreats to St. Joseph's Solitude, a retreat house on the Notre Dame campus. It's a quiet place — a place where I can close the door. People in retreats have just let me in when I was on the brink of mind destruction. It's places like the back pew and the Solitude as well as the people affiliated with the Catholic church that have nurtured me and allowed me to flow freely.

As I look back on the faith, and my growth, my belief is steadfast. I believe that the Lord is Jesus Christ and in the end we will all answer. I know that somehow he'll weigh out my whole person and will not hold me to my past sins. I believe that he's a forgiving guy. He is mercy. And I'm thankful for that.

These are my feelings and my own personal reflections of what it's like to be a black lay spiritual Christian woman. My music has taken me through so much. It's my gift to those who can hear it. It's the pain and the joy that I feel. If it's the end, the Lord will make a way. We have to hold on and we have to ask the Lord to have mercy. These are all songs and feelings that have been a part of my spiritual growth.

Even though we hurt and we suffer still in the life that we live, we have to take off and pull back. We have to take the time that we need to re-evaluate ourselves, but not to question our faith — that has to be steadfast. We have to fix our minds on what's right and do it the best we can. I used to think that on your knees with your hands folded was the only way to pray. Now I find it wonderfully relaxing to sit in my bed and to ask the Lord to come into my life and show me what he has for me.

Quiet time is important. You have to have a door with a lock and key to do this. I usually didn't have that so I'd have to pull out to one of these retreats. I was always welcomed with open arms. They took care of me and let me feel like a person so that my growth and my faith has come from the Catholic church as well as the Catholic people — lay and religious.

My faith tells me that I'm a person. I'm a black, Catholic, Christian lay woman who really cares about the church because the church has cared for me. When I say the Catholic church, I really mean the people of the Catholic church, the St. A's community, who nurtured my faith.

They've been there to assure me. Support like that en-
riches your faith. I've prayed this prayer steadily for a
couple of years: "I don't believe you're doing all this for
me, Lord. I don't believe that I'm here. I'm here because
I believe in you, and I'm the best I can be under the cir-
cumstances."

•

Every morning I have a ritual that I've been doing for the
past four years and it really strengthens me. I get up about
5:45. I sit in the middle of my bed and I light my candle
and I have a list of readings for the day. I try to do that
all the time wherever I am. I light the candle and read
the readings, and then I lay down and look at the flame
and reflect on what the readings mean to me. What part
of that reading can I take with me today as I get ready to
start on a new journey.

Then I start off with my own blessings, the things that
I'm most thankful for. As I look at my sleeping sons I'm
thankful that they are as well as they are. I'm thankful
for my parents who are still well and for all the people
who I really care about and for all my dear friends. Then
I ask for peace in the world. Then I can go out and do
some good for one or two people. Lately, it's the children
who I have been working with. I sit and listen and see if
anything's being said to me or if I'm being called to do
anything.

I think that there's no formal way to pray. Sometimes,
I sit in the middle of my bed and I say, "You know, Lord,
I know you're busy and I know that there are about 20
million more of these prayers coming up to you, but if
somehow you could find yourself free to hear a sinner's
prayer. I know that I have sinned, and I'm willing to
make amends for it by being the best person I can be.

We need a break, we need someone to hire people, poor people need to earn some money, they need some way to be motivated." I pray that maybe there could be some kind of motivator that could get everyone's wheels turning and everyone could come together somehow to make jobs.

I just pray for faith. I leave every morning with some kind of hope in my heart. Maybe hope that nothing will happen to my kids or anybody that I love. Or hope that the day goes well. Then I sit back and say, "Yeah, the bills are paid, that's good." I congratulate myself for accomplishments well done. I think, "Great, you paid all the bills on time, you didn't bounce a check, the kids have their basic needs, and there's food." Then I begin to feel the person I am. I have a right. I'm working in the system. I'm coming into the system with an excellent insight into what it is to be on the other end of the spectrum — to be poor and on the margins of society.

●

As I look at the seasons change this year, I see I've had a chance to travel, and a chance to grow from MayLee with the mind that everyone is out to get you, everyone is going to hurt you and use you and take from you. That was so insecure. I'm moving slowly. I'm not there yet, but I'm moving slowly in that direction of claiming my rights for myself.

My faith journey has been incredible. The music that I sing and the songs that I've made up make me think of Harriet Tubman and Soldier Matrusse. They always walked and prayed and sang. They never stopped singing. I have to sing too. That's part of my faith — my faith journey. It's because I've been all the way to the bottom and I know what the bottom tells me. My faith tells me that I don't have to stay there. It's easy to sit there and say, "God doesn't like me. God's not sending me any blessings."

I'm so amazed. I believe that with all the things that happen to us, God gives us just enough to come back. I think about myself, and I used to think, "I'm not going to do any better. God don't care about no black woman nohow." I used every excuse to say that God didn't care. But, maybe it's me. I always thought that there was something wrong with me, that I wasn't good enough. But now that I've had a chance to travel and talk with people and meet people, I realize that it's in your mind. People have to come to terms with themselves and accept who they are. I looked myself over in the mirror and I thought, "Most of this weight and all, MayLee, is part of you. What you don't like you have to do something about. You have to work hard." As I've looked and grown, and as I've come from the bottom up, it hasn't been a quick process. It's been a long struggle. You learn things along the way about yourself, about others, about what is needed to make this world a little more stable.

•

Since I was a young child, I knew that there was something good about me. I knew that there was something kind about me. I didn't always get nurtured with that so I wasn't really secure with that. It's still sometimes a problem with me to understand. I pray that I become stronger and become the best person that I can be. I'm not beyond thinking that I could become a theology teacher. I have the history of black Catholics under my belt, which is a dynamic tool.

I know that I'm not what I used to be. I know that I haven't reached the full potential of what I can be, and I'm going to keep trying. I'm not the type of Christian who goes around saying, "Look what the Lord has done for me. Let me show you." But if I were to get into a conversation with someone who wanted me to tell them, I certainly could.

I believe in Jesus' method. He went around and he healed people, and he kept a low profile. He didn't want everybody knocking on the door and congratulating him. He took it humble. Being a poor person and having suffered, I can be humble. It's no problem for me to break down and say "I'm sorry," or "Thank you," or "I made a mistake and I apologize for it." It's not beyond me to apologize for a mistake. The kids that I misjudge in my work, I just break down and tell them I'm sorry. I'm not even close to perfect. But know that I care.

I'm trying to be the best I can be. The readings and the scripture and just seeing Jesus — these are my role models. I can see Jesus. I can see all these people with two fish and five loaves of bread. In my work we have taken little or nothing and fed many. It can be done, but you have to believe and you have to suffer and you have to wait it out. You have to pray.

•

I've been so afraid in my life. I sometimes didn't know if I would live or die. I think there is an ultimate point in your life when you have to make some kind of decision. Each time that I've made the decision, it's been a good decision because each time I grew a little more. It was slow tracks, but eventually God's unchanging hand would just come there and tip me back over on the right side.

I don't feel no way tired,
I've come too far from where I started from,
Nobody told me the road would be easy,

But I don't believe he brought me this far just to leave
*   me,*
Pray for me, I'll pray for you,
and between the combination prayers
and everybody in the world,
God is good.

God will show us the right way. God showed me.